WHALES OF
WORLD WAR II

Military Life of Robert Jagers
June 1942 to October 1945

Written by:

ROBERT B. JAGERS

En-Joy

Bob Jagers

LST 351

Whales of World War II
© Copyright 2000; 2003; 2010 by Robert Jagers

First Edition -- Published May 2000
Second Printing -- August 2003
Third Printing -- September 2010

Robert Jagers
3712 Viewmont Dr.
Carrollton, TX 75007
BJagers@greatid.com

Military life of Robert Jagers,
June 1942 to October 1945 - US Navy
Amphibious Fleet, LST

180 p. : ill., maps ; 22 cm, English
Includes bibliographical references (p. 161) and index

LC Classification D769.45.J34 2000
Dewey Class 940.54/59/092 B 21
Library of Congress LCCN 2002-280198
ISBN 978-0-9744743-0-4

Dedicated to the Sailors of the Amphibious Forces of *World War II*

Acknowledgments

I wish to thank Nancy McCoy for giving me the encouragement to write of my experiences, Bill Smith, Phil Mohan, Jim White, and my daughter Kathleen Downs for their grammar corrections; and John Sheridan for his assistance regarding photograph copyright regulations. I would also like to thank my daughter Beverly Foley for her pointing out the dubious to the landlubbers, my son Richard for his computer support, digital editing and layout work. Mike McCormick, Phil Lubliner and Dennis Zaleski for their electronic and computer assistance, Jan Laurencelle and Cindy Cordle for their digital graphics work, Jennifer Politi for her generating readable map sections from the crude maps created by the author, James Roush and Alan Shippey for their artistic work for the cover. Most of all my faithful friend and wife, Rose, for putting up with me for the time it took to put this book together.

Preface

There was a prophet from Geth in Galilee, his name was Jonah. God commanded Jonah to go to Nineveh, a wicked city in Assyria and announce its destruction. Jonah sought to evade this task and fled in the opposite direction. He embarked from Joppa for Tarshish.

There was an extremely severe storm while he was at sea. The sailors were very frightened and believed that someone was aboard their ship that did not belong. There was a myth at that time which the sailors believed, "if someone strange was on board their ship that a terrible storm would develop." The captain searched the ship and found Jonah asleep in the hold. Jonah confessed that he was fleeing from the wicked city of Nineveh. He told the sailors that he was wrong and that he was the cause of the storm. He also explained to them that if they would throw him into the sea; the storm would abate. So the sailors cast him into the waters and the sea became calm.

However, God wished that Jonah complete his assignment. So He arranged for a large fish with a huge mouth to swallow Jonah. While Jonah was in the belly of the whale he realized his mistakes. He cried out to the Lord to save him. The Lord heard his plea and caused the fish to deposit Jonah safely on the shore. The Lord then repeated His command to Jonah. He entered Nineveh and preached penance, threatening destruction if his message went unheeded. The city repented and was saved.

The **Whales of World War II** were also called upon to deposit men safely on the shores of the enemy. Men and equipment were loaded at one shore then transferred to another shore by the ships with the large mouth (open bow doors) and a huge belly (tank deck). These ships became a vital and important factor in the defeat of the Germans and the Japanese during World War II. These modern **Whales of World War II** were called **LSTs (Landing Ship Tanks)**.

The author spent two years aboard the LST 351 in the European Theater of Operations. This LST ship participated in four invasions and five major engagements during this time.

Landing Ship Tanks (LST)- LST 351 the author's ship and home for 2 years.

WHALES OF WORLD WAR II

Pre-enlistment

I was attending Aquinas College in Grand Rapids, Michigan when the Japanese bombed Pearl Harbor in December 1941. I was in my sophomore year studying engineering. It was late March or early April 1942 when a friend of mine from school asked me to go with him to the Air Force recruitment center. We went and listened to the officer, who wanted to have us both enlist immediately. I said I would have to think about it. The officer said that I would have an excellent opportunity to become an officer and a pilot because of my two years of college pre-engineering. My friend returned later and enlisted in the Air Force. He became a pilot and flew a bomber in the Pacific. He flew his twenty to twenty-five missions and returned to the states.

Enlisting in the Naval Reserve

As a youth, I had been in the Boy Scouts and later the Sea Scouts. The Sea Scouts are similar to the Boy Scouts except the badges, studies, etc. are related more to the water. This prompted me to join the Navy. I enlisted in the Navy in April 1942 before I received my draft notice and a few days after my friend joined the Air Force. The Navy officer at the recruitment office informed me that I could finish my semester at college before I received my orders. He told me that the Navy would inform me of the time and place to report for active duty. I completed the semester, and shortly thereafter I received my notice to report to the Great Lakes Naval Training Center north of Chicago, Illinois.

"Boot Camp"

I left Grand Rapids in June 1942 and traveled to Chicago by train. The Navy assigned me to company number 477 under the guidance of Steve Belechick. Steve was a former pro football player who played fullback. His son is presently the defensive coordinator for the professional football team, the New York Jets.

The Navy wanted us to be in top physical condition. We marched, we ran, we studied the Blue Jacket Manual, and we had rifle practice. We went over and through an obstacle course many times. One of the items in the obstacle course was a seven-foot wall. We had to scale this wall and drop to the other side. This was very easy for me as I was a spry 5 ft 7 in tall and weighed 130 pounds. It was my function to give the others a boost with my folded hands. Then it would be my turn to scale the wall. I would get a running start, jump against the wall and reach for the top and pull myself over to the other side.

There were three facets of our training that seemed most important:

1. physical fitness--this was accomplished by calisthenics (sit ups, jumping jacks, pull ups, running, marching sometimes with all of our gear) and naturally the obstacle course; Another part of the training was a rope climbing exercise. You had to climb hand over hand to the top of a vertical rope, (approximately twenty feet) and then slide down to the bottom. I became the winner many times this was due to my competitive nature, coupled with my strength and agility. We would race two or more persons at one time. The ropes were hanging side by side from a horizontal pipe. Then the winners would compete against each other. This meant that the winner had to do more climbs than any other person. Some of the lazy ones would just give up during the first climb. Then they did not have to exert themselves any more than was necessary.

2. discipline and respect--accomplished by threat of punishment and general common sense;

3. the making of a sailor--accomplished by the reading of the Blue Jacket Manual; this included learning gunnery and the breakdown and reassembling of different weapons, knot tying, and many other items necessary to make sailors out of these green horns.

The Navy barber gave us our haircuts. We heard many stories and rumors regarding our future haircuts, i.e., a bowl would be placed on your head and the hair was cut around the bowl (this is what our haircuts actually looked like). Another story was that they would take your sailor's hat and toss it into the air and your hair would be cut before it came down, (this is also a fair description). The Navy did everything on a mass production basis: showers, laundry, meals, etc.

A Sailor's Sea Bag
and His Sleeping Gear

Many times during boot camp we marched with our hammock, mattress and our full sea bag. A sailor's sea bag was his suitcase. It held everything the sailor owned. The sea bag was made from canvas and was about three feet high and a little over twelve inches in diameter.

The top had several brass eyelets. It was closed with a rope passing through the eyelets and this gear package weighed almost 100 pounds. Part of our assigned gear included our hammock. The hammock and mattress were rolled to form a "U" and wrapped around the top of the sea bag.

Hammocks became our bed for a long time starting with our first day at "Boot Camp." These were hung between two-four inch pipes. Some of the fellows could not adjust to the hammocks and kept falling out and we would hear the thumps when they hit the floor. There were usually two or three thumps every night for the first two weeks. We were constantly moving during our daytime training and never had sufficient sleep.

Physical Examinations

We also had our physical that included a series of shots. What a production line it was! We walked between two lines of medical personnel. We received a dab of alcohol, then a shot in the right arm. We took a few more steps and this procedure was repeated for the left arm until each person received five or six shots. Some of the men fainted. This was partially due to the inexperienced medical personnel administering the inoculations. There were many sore arms and a few bent needles. A dentist examined our teeth and X-rays were taken.

There is another military term that I will mention here: it is called "short arm inspection." The explanation of this terminology may seem crude to some but to others a source of humor. A "short arm inspection" is the examination of a man's private parts for any insects, lice, or signs of a venereal disease. It was during a "short arm inspection" at the Great Lakes Training Center that an extremely humorous event occurred. This particular day the doctors and medics were searching for insects. The man behind me was a very tall person from Kentucky. He was scratching himself rather vigorously. The medic looked at him and asked what was his problem? The Kentuckian answered, "I do not know if I have a million of those critters or just one on a motorcycle." Every man within hearing distance just roared. Each man was sprayed or dusted with a powder as he passed a certain point.

Swimming Requirement

There was one important requirement that was impressed upon the sailors. That requirement was that all sailors must be able to swim fifty yards. There is a very strong reason for this distance. There is a very strong eddy current suction when a ship sinks. It was determined that fifty yards was a safe distance to avoid this suction.

I was pushed off a pier when I was a nine-year old boy. I did not know how to swim. Those older boys thought it was a big laugh that they could pick on me. This event instilled in me a fear of water. I carried this fear with me to adulthood. The swimming instructor at the Great Lakes Naval Training Center apparently realized my situation. He said if I would learn the side stroke, it would help me overcome this fear. He taught me the side stroke. He also explained why this method of swimming would help me. He stated that with the side stroke it was easier and simpler to keep one's head above water. I practiced and practiced the side stroke. I easily passed the minimum distance. Today, I continue to use this swimming method. I also overcame my fear of the water.

Quartermaster-Signalman School

I was assigned to the Quartermaster-Signaling school. I believe I was assigned to this school because of my Scouting experience. The signaling part dealt with the transfer of information by some visual means. The quartermaster part of the training dealt with the steering of the ship, log entries, reading charts and plotting one's position. It was in this school that we learned Morse code, the semaphore system, a method of sending a visual messages utilizing two flags held in various positions. Fortunately for me I already had an excellent knowledge of both the Morse code and the semaphore system. I learned both systems of communication as a Boy Scout. We also studied the identification and meaning of the flags in the international flag system.

The semaphore system is responsible for the present day peace symbol. The new peace symbol was determined from two letters in the semaphore system. The two letters are "N" and "D." The symbol and the letters stand for "nuclear deterrent." The "D" is designated with one arm straight up and the other straight down. The "N" is determined with the arms down at 45 degrees one on each side.

Ship and airplane identifications were some of the other subjects that were taught during the intensive training. Some of the other subjects we studied were: how to enter information into the ship's log, celestial navigation, the compass, star charts, navigation charts, tides, dead reckoning, and depth sounding. Depth sounding is a system of determining the water depth by casting a weighted line into the water. The line has several knots spaced at definite intervals to identify the amount of rope in the water and thus determine the depth. We studied many different knots.

Liberty

Every other weekend the sailors were given liberty (this is the name for a sailor's free time away from the base or ship). I usually went to Chicago since I had many relatives living there and it was relatively close to the naval base. The train ride from Great Lakes Training Center to Chicago took about seventy minutes. I also had a place to stay if I was fortunate to receive over-night liberty. One clever sailor (during one of these liberties) would bet on the flip of a quarter. It seemed that he figured exactly how the coin would land. He would correctly call "heads or tails." He earned his spending money in this manner.

Choice of Duty

Our commanding officer suggested that we select the types of ships that were of most interest to us; battleships: submarines, destroyers, cruisers, etc. We made our selection before our graduation from the Quartermaster-Signaling school. I opted for submarine training. They gave me a very thorough psychological examination and an exhaustive written test. They also tested me for the fear of claustrophobia. Submarine living meant that we would be in close contact with each other and in extremely close and confined quarters. The number of persons needed for the next group was twenty. If any one of the previous twenty were rejected or changed their mind, then I would be the next person assigned to submarine duty. I was number 21 on the list. It just so happened that all twenty were selected and I was then left without a choice of type of ship. I now realize how foolish and brash I was at age twenty.

Amphibious Training

I received orders at the end of November 1942 to report to the Amphibious Training School in Solomons, Maryland after I completed the Quartermaster-signaling training course. It was determined that I would be a signalman rather than a quartermaster. I believe that my proficiency in both semaphore and Morse code led to this decision. I would have preferred the other rating as I felt it would be more interesting and challenging.

I wonder why they called this a school. It was definitely the mud hole of the world. We had a very difficult time keeping clean, especially our clothes. We were taught more signaling, more navigation, an unusual amount of gunnery training including the breakdown and reassembling of a 20 mm cannon while blindfolded. The training was very intensive with considerable emphasis on the identification of German, French, English, and American planes and warships. This gave us a strong clue that we were probably going to Europe.

Christmas Leave

We had several months of strenuous and intensive training when we were told that we could have four days leave for Christmas 1942; at the time of the announcement concerning the leave, I was out of funds. I had a large portion of my sailor's pay deducted to be sent home to my mother. I went to the chaplain and asked him if there was any way I could get the money to go home (such as the Red Cross). The Solomons base was in such a remote area that I knew it would be extremely difficult to make any contact with the Red Cross. The Chaplain agreed with me that it would be extremely difficult to obtain any funds from the Red Cross. However, he said he would lend the money to me and, possibly, I could pay him back when I returned.

We left the base in an LST (Landing Ship Tank). The planning and the logistics of a war can be mind boggling. It was slightly more than one year since Pearl Harbor and over three hundred LSTs were built before we were granted this Christmas leave. Who knew in advance that we would need this type of ship and when?

This was also my first sailing adventure. There were three to four hundred men on this LST. They placed us in the tank deck. It was cold and extremely damp. We sailed to Baltimore, Maryland where we were able to make our connections. The distance from Solomons to

Fig 1. A side view of an LST. This is similar to the ship in which I sailed from Solomons to Baltimore.

Baltimore is approximately fifty miles. The ride took several hours.

I took a train to Detroit from Baltimore; two of my buddies went on to Chicago. I took the bus from the Detroit train station to the end of the bus line on Grand River Avenue. I think it went as far as Farmington which is about 20 miles NW from Detroit. My destination was Grand Rapids which was an additional 150 miles. There did not seem to be any transportation to Grand Rapids other than hitchhiking. So I started to hitchhike to Grand Rapids. The first ride I was able to get took me to Lansing. The car could not go very fast and there was no heater. I thought I was going to freeze to death. Then from Lansing I received another ride and then a third and finally arrived in Grand Rapids at about 0300 (3 AM).

I thought that it would take a month to thaw out my cold aching body. However, spending one night in a bed with the proper covers and then eating my mother's home cooking, and I was feeling great the next day. We were advised not to say anything about our training or where we were based. All we could say was that we were going through Navy training in Maryland. It was very difficult not to divulge more than this as my relatives were constantly asking many questions. We could talk about our base, and living quarters, but we were not to mention any names or any definite location nor could we talk about the type of training.

Concern for Shipmates Creates an Awkward Situation

I hitchhiked to Chicago from Grand Rapids to catch the train back to Baltimore. It was relatively easy to obtain a ride as I was in my uniform. People were eager to give a military person a ride provided he was in uniform. I also met my two buddies at the train station in Chicago. They brought a bottle of whiskey with them. They told me that the bottle was to help them keep warm. I think it was to help them forget. They were nipping at this bottle all the way to Pittsburgh where we had to change trains for Baltimore. They were feeling pretty good by the time we reached Pittsburgh. I was very concerned about them and made sure they had their tickets and all of their belongings. We boarded the train to Baltimore. I realized that in the confusion I did not have my ticket. I had left it in the slot at the back of the seat. I jumped off the train and headed for the previous one so I could recover my ticket from the slot at the back of the seat. The conductor had already taken my ticket. I looked out the window and saw that the train to Baltimore was moving. I jumped off and started to run to catch the train. A railroad man stepped in my path and kept me from going any farther. This left me in the Pittsburgh railroad station without any money, no identification, no winter coat and no known means of continuing on to Baltimore. I spoke to several railroad employees about my situation with no results. Then I met an official who said he would see what could be done to get me to Baltimore.

This railroad official made arrangements for me to take the next train to Baltimore, which left Pittsburgh about 2 hours after the original train. I had to ride in the passageway between two railroad cars, in a standing position. I almost froze as I did not have my pea coat with me. The pea coat is a sailor's winter coat. My coat plus my other belongings including my identification were on the other train with my two buddies. I finally arrived in Baltimore and went to the pier where the LST was docked. I had arrived in time to catch the ship back to the base. However, since I did not have my ID, I was not permitted to board the ship. What do I do now?

I decided to look for my friends and searched the waterfront bars but could not find them. It was very cold in Baltimore and I had no hat, no coat, nor identification. I was soon picked up by the Baltimore police. The police believed that I was AWOL (Absent With Out Leave) However, they accepted my explanation. They drove me around in the police cruiser looking for my friends but without success. The police finally dropped me near my ship. Just as they were pulling up the gangplank my buddies appeared. They had sobered up enough to remember to bring my coat, my hat, and my gear. I returned to the base feeling much better. The coldness of the tank deck on the return trip did not bother me as much as the incoming trip. I was able to repay the Chaplain for my trip home with some money given to me by my relatives.

Ship Board Training

This very intensive training continued until we were ordered to board LST 323 for some actual sea experience in January or February 1943. There were three crews in training at one time plus the regular crew. We did most of our training in the Chesapeake Bay and finally ventured out into the Atlantic Ocean. The experience that we gained while sailing the Chesapeake Bay prepared us for this eventual jaunt into the Atlantic Ocean. Our initial incursion on the training ship was exhilarating, especially to someone from the Midwest.

Spinal Meningitis

We were returning to the base from a training session when one of the training crew members became very sick. It was determined that he had spinal meningitis and had to be taken to a hospital immediately.

This man departed with a small boat crew, a corpsman, a signalman and an officer. A corpsman is a person with some medical training but not enough to be a doctor. Many of the civilian pharmacists became hospital corpsmen when they were assigned to their functions. They would have studied at a hospital corpsman school. Their knowledge of medicine would be beneficial. The signalman would be familiar with Morse code. He would be able to send or receive any messages if necessary.

Shortly thereafter, another man became ill with the same disease. Another boat crew was ordered to take this sick sailor to the hospital. Again there had to be an officer, a corpsman, and a signalman. I was selected as the signalman to accompany this crew. We started towards the shore in the middle of the night (remember we could not use any lights nor were there any lights on shore). Originally we were going to head directly towards the shore and follow it to the channel opening leading to our base. The officer in charge of our boat decided to take a short cut. He ordered the coxswain (the leader of the boat crew) to head across the bay.

We were underway much longer than we had anticipated. We finally found the shore. We eventually entered an unknown channel that we followed until we came to a small private dock. This dock belonged to a local farmer.

The farmer informed us that the closest Navy base was the Patuxent Naval Air Station. This base was notified and an ambulance was dispatched to the farm. The officer, the corpsman and the sick person were placed in the ambulance. The ambulance driver informed us that they were going to the Patuxent Naval Air Base. The boat crew and I were left to shift for ourselves.

The farmer gave us waterway directions to the Naval Air Station. We continued up this channel until we reached the Naval Air Base. We spoke to the officer at the base and found that we were across the inlet from our original destination. That officer's shortcut really got us lost. It was a fortunate trick of fate that we were lost, as the facilities at the Naval Air Base were considerably better than they were at our base. We spent the night at the Patuxent Naval Air Base and the next morning we were able to return to our ship.

We were wondering why we were not placed in quarantine because of the nature of this disease. Later, we heard that the first man had died from his disease but the sailor that sailed with us had lived.

Quarantine at a Coal Dock

This dreadful disease meant that the ship had to be quarantined until the disease could run its course. Our ship was moved to an old coal loading dock near Norfolk, Virginia. Several doctors came aboard plus several more hospital corpsmen. These additional people would also be quarantined until the doctors determined that it was safe to return the ship back to its normal functions. We were over four hundred persons on a ship equipped to handle one hundred. Throat cultures were taken from everyone every day and examined. This is the manner of checking for occurrence of the disease affecting any additional persons. Fortunately, no one else showed signs of this disease but we had to wait the required twenty-one days to complete the quarantine time. Our mail was delivered to the end of the dock and we had to go and get it ourselves. There could not be any outgoing mail. No one was

Fig 2. This photo illustrates the variety of vehicles that can be loaded onto the top deck of an LST.

permitted to come aboard. No one was allowed to leave (including all the extra medical personnel we had on board). We loaded our garbage on the huge elevator. This elevator's normal function was to raise and lower the mobile vehicles to and from the top deck to the tank deck.

Elevator Accident

The garbage was taken to the end of the dock where persons dressed in special protective clothing would gather it and immediately burn it.

It was during one of these garbage pickups that we had a very bad accident. It had been loaded with garbage and there were about fifteen to twenty persons on the elevator. Someone had removed the

Fig 3. This photo illustrates the versatility of an LST. Here it is being used to transport vehicles up a river. The circular stacks seen are air ducts to the engine room.

retaining pins on the top deck elevator. This resulted in a sudden drop of the elevator platform when the gears were disengaged. There were several persons with broken bones; many others had cuts, or severe bruises. These injuries were the direct result of the falling elevator.

These injuries plus the presence of the garbage were not a very pleasant occurrence.

We could not take on board any more medical personnel. Therefore, we had to manage our problems with the people that were already on board. Every person was asked to offer assistance in whatever manner he or she could. I had considerable experience in dealing with injured persons through my Scout training. I also had several courses in Red Cross first aid training. Therefore, I was able to bandage some of the injuries, put on temporary splints, treat cuts and abrasions, administer morphine, and give blood plasma.

Formation of a New Crew

We were finally released from the quarantine after 21 days. We returned to our base at Solomons, Maryland.

Ninety (90) enlisted men and ten (10) officers were selected and instructed to form a new crew. A new LST would be assigned to us. The formal name of our type of ship was **LANDING SHIP TANKS** or **LST**. The soldiers that traveled on our ships fondly called them "Long Slow" or "Large Slow Targets." The sailors had another nickname for these flat bottom ships: "A Lot of Shit and Trouble."

The number of our LST was 351. There were many of these LSTs built at various locations in the United States. The final count exceeded (1100). Therefore, the LSTs were given a number in lieu of a name. We took aboard minimal supplies.

Shakedown Cruise

We sailed out into the Atlantic Ocean for our shakedown cruise. This was to determine if everything was functioning properly. We sailed for several days. It also allowed each person in this new crew to become familiar with the equipment and areas that would fall within their responsibility. It also allowed everyone to become acquainted with his fellow ship-mates. Our training cruise in the Chesapeake Bay prepared us for entering the Atlantic Ocean. We wondered if this brand new ship would hold together. Here we were entering this huge body of water without any ones assistance. It felt that we had the world at our feet.

Supplies Received in New York

We sailed for New York. The balance of our shakedown cruise was continued on our journey to New York City.

All the supplies that we would need to outfit our ship would be ready for us in the port of New York at pier 92. We were given a very long list of materials to turn over to the proper authorities in New York.

How Large Is A Can Of Powdered Milk?

One of the items we became accustomed to during our training cruise was powdered milk. This powdered milk came in cans that weighed approximately ten pounds. Our master supply list stated that we should order ten cans of powdered milk. Our storekeeper felt that ten cans or approximately 100 pounds would not last very long so he changed the order to read one hundred cans. Imagine our surprise when the cans we ordered contained approximately one hundred pounds of powdered milk! Therefore, we had about 10,000 pounds of powdered milk instead of the expected 1000 pounds. We had difficulty finding storage places for all of these extra cans. I think that every available space was used to store these cans. This even meant that several cans would be stored in the flag locker on the main deck.

The flag locker was part of my responsibility. The flag locker was a horizontal storage area for our flags used in our communications system, including the International flags. Two years later when we decommissioned the ship we still had some of this original order of powdered milk.

We spent several days in New York. It took this long to complete outfitting and supplying our ship. I am not a drinking person but some of our crewmembers secretly plotted to take me into New York and get me drunk. We visited several bars and I had my drink. I slowly sipped mine while they were having two or three drinks. The same thing happened at the next bar. They had six or eight drinks while I had less than three. Guess who got drunk? They never tried this again.

Meaning of Censorship

We finally received all the necessary supplies and were given orders to join a convoy and we sailed for Bermuda. This trip took another several days. It was approximately the middle of March 1943 when we arrived in Bermuda. A few sailors were given liberty, but I was not one of the lucky ones. Some of the men had written home and said the onions were very delicious. They were referring to Bermuda onions. The censoring officer promptly deleted this reference.

We were in Bermuda for several days waiting for a convoy to be organized including the escorts. The escort ships for a convoy usually consisted of some DDs (destroyers) and DDEs (destroyer escorts) The escort ships were there to protect the convoy from submarines.

These ships had the underwater detection equipment to determine the presence and the location of any submarines. The escorts also had the depth charges that were the principle attack weapon against the German

Fig 4. A destroyer escort (DDE). These ships were very fast and possessed equipment to detect and damage enemy submarines.

U-boats. The U-boat was the name given to the submarines, sort of an acronym for underwater boat. The depth charges would be rolled off a rack on the stern of the ship. Sometimes the depth charges would be fired from a Y gun. Those fired from the Y gun would be sent to either side while the rack charges would drop into the water astern of the escort. It was not necessary for the depth charges to hit the submarine. The exploding charges caused an extreme pressure increase in the water. This pressure wave was so great that it could damage the hull of the submarine, resulting in a leak or a hole in the U-Boat. The severity of the damage would determine the action to be taken by the submarine commander.

Speed of an LST

The LST is the slowest moving of all the ships in the convoy. Our normal convoy speed was 5 to 6 knots (approximately six miles per hour).

The convoy could only move as fast as the normal cruising speed of the slowest ships; thus the convoy could only travel as fast as our ship. Some of the other convoys that did not include LSTs would travel at ten to twelve knots.

Fig 5. A destroyer (DD). These ships were very fast and possessed equipment to detect and damage enemy submarines. The destroyer has more armament and is better equipped. They provided protection to the convoy as they crossed the ocean.

The command ship would relay orders that the convoy had to zigzag, to reduce the possibility of submarines determining our course and speed. It was difficult for a convoy of 50 or 60 ships to zigzag at

Fig 6. LSTs zigzagging in a convoy. Note: the barrage balloons and the very small destroyer escort at the top.

the same time without a collision; the timing of the beginning of a turn and the degree of the turn were critical. The lowering of a flag from the command ship indicated the moment this maneuver was to start..

It took thirty-six days for us to cross the Atlantic Ocean, due to the zigzag course we were forced to observe and to the very slow speed of the LSTs.

Watches and Bells

The time a sailor is officially on duty is called a watch. These are normally four hours long. A sailor is on watch for four hours then off watch for eight hours. If this system were to continue then a sailor would be on watch the same time every day. It is desirable to upset this continuing the same watch. This is accomplished by taking the watch from 4 PM (1600 hours) to 8 PM (2000 hours) and dividing it into two watches. These two hour watches are called "dog watches." It is a form of staggering the times you are officially on duty.

Our crew decided to work four-hour shifts while crossing the Atlantic Ocean. Therefore, there would not be any "dog watches." I ended up with the twelve to four (1200 hours to 1600 hours) watch both in the afternoon and at midnight (2400 hours to 0400 hours).

There is a system of bells used on every ship sailing the seas. This system consists of ringing a bell every half hour starting at 12:30 AM (0030 hours). One bell would be rung at this time One more bell (two bells) would be rung at the next half hour. This continues until eight bells are rung. The bells were rung in groups of two. It is not necessary to count the number of bells rung as the ringing in twos simplifies the counting. A sailor hearing the number of bells plus identifying the specific watch, he then knew the time of the day.

The hours in parentheses are military time. A sailor hearing the number of bells plus knowing the name of the particular watch then realizes the time of the day or night. This is necessary because during a 24 hour period the bells are rung the same six times a day. Two bells of the "graveyard watch" signifies 1 AM (0100 hours).

Entering North African Waters

We sailed eastward and crossed the Atlantic Ocean. We passed the rock of Gibraltar about the end of April 1943 without any problems. A few ships had to leave the convoy for some mechanical problems; mostly, related to the engines. These mechanical problems caused the troubled ships to straggle and they had to leave the convoy. Generally, there would not be any escort ships to stay and protect these stragglers.

These stragglers then became easy targets for any lurking submarine.

A submarine wolf pack is made up of several U-boats. This group of submarines would enter the middle of a convoy submerged. They could fire their torpedoes at any of the ships because the ships could not fire back for fear of hitting other ships in the convoy. The escorts could not enter into the center of the convoy due to the nature of positioning the ships. These wolf packs were creating considerable havoc on some of the convoys crossing the Atlantic Ocean.

The landing in North Africa by American troops had taken place earlier. The code name for this operation was "TORCH." The British were fighting the Germans and General Rommel in the east. The invasion by the American troops at Casablanca in the west began a pincers movement towards the Germans.

We entered the port of Oran, Algeria where we took on fresh water, food, and other miscellaneous supplies. There were two French warships in the harbor. The political situation between the allies and the French government created some uneasy moments as we entered the harbor. We were not sure if the French naval ships would fire at us.

Some of the British warships had some French sailors on board. The Americans and the British warships did not wish to fire upon the French Navy; therefore, a radio message was sent to the French fleet. The message stated, "If you will point your search lights skyward then there will not be any firing at the French ships." Apparently, the French Navy did not receive this message. Consequently, there was some initial firing by the allied ships. This occurred at the port of Casablanca and also at Oran. The French warships surrendered immediately. It was obvious to them that it was a lost cause to return the fire. Therefore, everything was settled at the time we entered the harbor at Oran. We made a brief stop at the port of Arzew after leaving Oran.

British Field Hospital

We left Oran and continued east. We stopped outside the town of Bougie, Algeria. It was at this time that I had several sharp pains in my right side. I was put ashore as the pharmacist mate thought I had appendicitis. I had to take my hammock, mattress, and sea bag. This would include all of my worldly belongings. It weighed between eighty and one hundred pounds. I was taken in a Jeep to a British field hospital.

This field hospital was located outside the town of Bougie. The entire hospital was in tents. I was told that there were over 3,000 patients there. I was the only American sailor. There were probably forty or fifty American injured soldiers in this hospital. The rest of the patients were mostly British who had been fighting in North Africa against the feared Afrika Corps under General Rommel.

I was put in a ward of twelve men. There was quite of lot of kidding and bantering among these British soldiers. One old timer (twelve years of service) was shot in the rear end and had to sleep on his stomach. He really took a lot of kidding from the other soldiers. Some of their remarks were: "why did you let that part of your body stick up?" or "did you not know enough to duck?" The British soldiers played some tricks on this veteran. They short-sheeted his bed. This meant he could not get all the way under the sheets. They also put some raw eggs in his bed on the day he was to be discharged. We all had a laugh when he sat on the eggs.

Several of the British soldiers in this first ward gave me their home addresses. I was able to visit their families later when I arrived in London. I actually dated the sister of one of these British friends. Her name was Joan Green. Joan came from Newcastle-on-Tyne. Joan and I corresponded with each other until 1964.

There was another soldier that I met while I was in the hospital. He came from Bromley, Kent. This is near London. I was able to visit this family later when our ship was ordered to England, while I was on liberty. Several years later (1955) my wife, two daughters and myself met the daughter of this family on a trip to Toronto, Canada.

British Tea and Coffee

The doctor determined that my medical situation was not immediately urgent. Therefore, he scheduled my operation to take place in two days. We were served tea eight times a day. We were served tea at breakfast, mid-morning, at noon, at two PM, at tea time (4:30PM), at dinner, at eight PM and before bedtime. This tea was watered down and served with powdered milk; no sugar nor lemon. I preferred my tea with lemon but it is obvious that I did not get my wish.

Each ward was supposed to receive two cups of coffee per man per week. We were informed that this was our ration allotment. Our particular ward never saw any of this allotted coffee.

There was a nurses' tent placed between two wards. You can imagine the degree of soundproofing these tent walls afforded. Therefore, we could hear what was taking place in the nurses' tent. Our allotment of coffee ended up in their tent. It was used to entertain their guests. Two nurses in our area were named Price. The soldiers soon nicknamed them "lower" and "higher price." This was determined by what could be overheard from the nurses' tent.

Appendix Operation

The day for my operation finally arrived. It was scheduled for 4:30 in the afternoon. I was taken into the first tent on a gurney and left there. Several minutes had elapsed at which time the nurse came in and informed me that my operation was going to be delayed so the doctor could have his tea. Tea time is extremely important for the British. It was rumored that the British lost a battle in North Africa because they had taken time out for their daily tea.

I asked the nurse what was the name and rank of the doctor? She told me that his rank was lieutenant colonel and his name was Butcher. What a name for a surgeon! I was wheeled into the operating theater (British term for operating room) which was another tent connected by a canvas cover to the first tent.

I lay on the operating table; a wire gauze strainer was placed over my mouth and nose. Liquid ether was poured onto this mask. I had my fingers on my chest and was moving them. I either stopped moving my fingers or I could not move them. I heard the doctor state "I think he has had enough" and the mask was removed. I received a breath of fresh African air and then sat up straight. The nurses had to start again with the anesthesia. The operation was completed and I was returned to my ward.

Then I became the butt of the English jokes, such as "since I had a cut in my side would I be eligible for the Purple Heart" or "why did I not keep my stomach down to avoid any bullet there." My incision was about ten inches long. (My wife's incision for her appendectomy performed in Argentina in 1971 was about one inch in length, in comparison). I can see why this doctor's name was Butcher.

Recovery

They eventually moved me into another ward for recuperation. I think there were thirty or forty men in this recovery ward. This was a much larger ward. We apparently did not require as much attention. A rather peculiar event happened to me after I was put into this ward. I was lying in bed with a bandage around my incision and wearing nothing else. One day the regular nurse came in and introduced me to a new trainee. The Sister (a British term for a commissioned officer nurse) was going to demonstrate to the trainee how to give a patient a bath. This poor trainee not knowing better pulled the sheet that was covering me all the way down to the end of the cot. I was fully exposed and the trainee became embarrassed. The senior nurse promptly informed her that you never fully expose a patient and showed her how to cover and bathe the patient one half at a time. I never saw that trainee again and inquired about her. I was informed that she had been transferred to another part of the hospital.

The war in North Africa officially ended on May 13, 1943. I was near the end of my recovery on this date.

British Movie Stars

Three movie stars came to the hospital to entertain the patients. I was invited to attend their performance. The stars were Vivian Leigh, Beatrice Lillie, and a male actor. I do not remember exactly the name of this actor. He was either Leslie Howard or Laurence Olivier. The performance of the stars took place in a long and narrow church like building. They performed a little skit. Bea Lillie went into the audience to speak with various persons. Bea Lillie would sit on a soldier's lap and crack jokes, or stroke his hair. The men simply loved every bit of this. She sang several songs. The British soldiers informed her that there was an American sailor in the audience. She asked "Where is this American sailor?" I stood up to be recognized. Bea Lillie came down the aisle and sang a song just for me. I was too far from the aisle for her to sit on my lap.

The male actor had some interesting stories to tell. Vivian Leigh did not do much other than her initial skit. Miss Leigh was very beautiful. It appeared that performing for the military was a boring chore for her. She just did not wish to mingle with the troops, but they adored her. It seemed that just appearing at the hospital was simply adequate in their eyes.

Beer Saves The Life of an American Soldier

There was an American soldier in the hospital who had burns over seventy percent of his body including many third degree burns. I was asked to talk to him, since I had healed sufficiently to walk around. I visited him every day, until it was time for my discharge from the hospital. He really looked forward to seeing me and having our daily chats. The doctors encountered a severe problem with this soldier. His burns were so severe that they could not feed him nor could they give him an IV (intravenous injection). It was determined that in his condition he needed nutrients and plenty of liquids. He was unable to take either. However, some bright doctor suggested that they try feeding him beer. This would provide some nutrients plus the much needed liquids. This was tried and proved to be very successful. The beer saved his life and permitted the doctors to do some skin grafting.

This soldier was on a continuous high from the beer. He was somewhat saddened when he heard that I was well enough to be discharged from the hospital. I was in that hospital for almost five weeks. A hot, humid, climate is not conducive to rapid healing.

Enemy Planes with An Eerie Noise

The Germans dive-bombed this hospital with their Stuka dive-bombers many times during the five weeks I was there, even though many of the tents were painted with a big red cross. It was in violation of the Geneva Convention. The Stuka created a very eerie noise during its dive. This was done deliberately to create fear in the enemy; the Germans drilled holes in the leading edge of the wings on these Stukas and the air passing through these leading edge holes is what created this whine.

Fig 7. A photo of the German dive-bomber, Stuka. Note: the fixed wheels and the gull like wing.

Train Ride to Beni Mancour

The time for my discharge from this British field hospital finally arrived. I was told I would be sent to Algiers by train and was given a railroad ticket and British traveling orders.

This ticket assured me passage to Algiers, but no farther. I was instructed that there would be a change in trains at Beni Mancour. I was given seven days rations on the day of my departure and told not to do any lifting for about two weeks (remember I had all of my gear that weighed almost 100 pounds). The seven days' rations included seven packages of hard tack (this is like a big soda cracker but extremely hard), seven tins of bully beef which is similar to corned beef, one package of tropical butter (probably would take a blow torch to melt it), and a package of tropical cheese that was very hard to cut even with a knife.

Fig 8. A sailor and his sea bag. This 100 pound package I was ordered not to lift, but I had to carry it.

My orders stated that I was to go to Algiers and meet the British RTO (Road Transportation Officer). The RTO was to give me orders to go to Oran. Oran being a naval base, the officers at Oran would know where my ship was located. There, I could receive transportation and connections to my ship or be placed on board another ship. My ship and many other LSTs were in Bizerte but I did not know this at the time of my discharge from the hospital.

Mixed Uniform

This was summer and it was very hot in the desert. My cooler white summer uniform was at the bottom of my sea bag and I did not wish to dump everything out to get at it. It is quite a job to pack the sea bag to get everything into it. It sometimes takes two or three attempts to pack everything into the sea bag properly. I was wearing my dark blue trousers, my white sailor's hat and a British army tan summer uniform shirt. The British summer shirt was obtained from a British soldier at the hospital. I could be reasonably cool dressed this way.

I rode in the passenger car for the first part of the train trip. The passengers included people, goats, chickens, ducks, and pigs. We arrived in Beni Mancour; it was approximately 100 miles from the Mediterranean Sea and about 150 miles from the hospital in Bougie (remember how I was dressed and that I had British orders). I was hungry so I traded with a native, one package of hard tack for some fresh eggs, just outside of the open air train station.

Gourmet Lunch

I started to build a fire outside the train station so that I could cook some of the eggs. I just had a nice fire going when the American military police (MPs) spotted me. I had to put out the fire and was arrested for being AWOL (absent without leave). They took me back to their base and I was put in front of the captain, the officer in charge. He apparently believed my story and apologized for the actions of his men. He said that his men had informed him that I was in the middle of my lunch when I was arrested. He said he did not have much to offer but I could have some of the American chow if I was interested. He offered me canned pork and beans and sliced canned pineapple. I ate very heartily and felt as if I had just been fed a gourmet meal; the food in the British hospital had not been very appetizing.

Ride to Algiers

His men took me back to the train station where I boarded the train bound for Algiers. This time I rode in the baggage car and was joined by three French soldiers.

We could not understand each other but enjoyed each other's company. Most of our communication was attained by the use of our hands. A few of the words in both English and French were similar. The Frenchmen would point out water or trees or anything that would inter-est me. We did a lot of gesturing. We passed the time by drinking some water or wine. I had the water and they had the wine. These soldiers introduced me to French claret. The ride in the baggage car was considerably more comfortable and less odoriferous than the ride in the

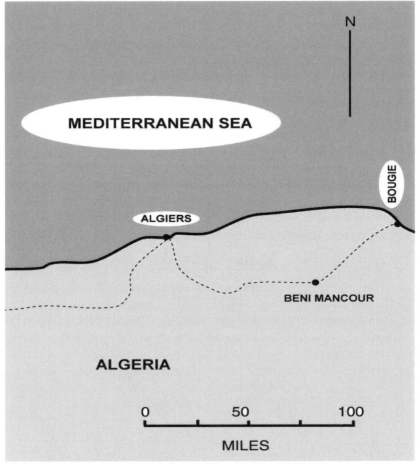

Fig 9. A map of North Africa showing the distance to the train stop at Beni Mancour and the balance of the train ride to Algiers.

passenger section. I finally reached my destination (Algiers), which was about 100 miles from Beni Mancour.

Where is the RTO?

I began to look for the RTO (Road Transportation Officer). No one knew of him or where he was located. I went to a park and built a fire and had a dinner of scrambled eggs, bully beef, and some tea. I had traded the tropical butter for some tea. Would you believe that the

British shipped me out without giving me any tea? I guess it was too precious for them.

I had not found the RTO by the time it became dark so I went down to the docks and located another LST. I requested permission to spend the night aboard. The officer in charge said OK and that I would have to leave after breakfast as they expected to sail then. I sure was looking forward to that breakfast. I was sound asleep when someone nudged me around 3 AM (0300) and informed me that I would have to leave as they had received sailing orders. I picked up my gear and went back to the park where I had been earlier. I curled up under a tree and awoke at dawn the next day.

I still could not find the RTO so I approached a Military Police post at a gate entering the city. The soldier in charge informed me that there were many vehicles passing through this gate and maybe he could find me a ride going west. The naval base at Oran is approximately 250 miles from Algiers. This city is almost on the western border of Algeria and Morocco. There at Oran, someone would be able to locate my ship or arrange to have me put aboard another LST.

The guard at this gate found me a ride with an ambulance traveling with a group of German prisoners. This particular motor convoy was headed for Oran where the prisoners were to be put aboard a ship. It seemed to suit my purpose of getting to Oran. It is amazing what a brash young sailor of twenty years will attempt.

Once, while the convoy was stopped for lunch a plane flew

Fig 10. A photo of the German fighter plane, an ME 109.

over us. It was an American P-51. This fighter plane, dubbed "Mustang" was a new addition to the allied aircraft, and had not been among the listed airplanes on our identification charts. The Mustang would distinguish itself as a long range fighter plane to help protect the

Fig 11. A silhouette comparison of an American P-51 (top) and a German ME 109 (bottom). It is easy to see why the German prisoners could mistake the identity of these 2 planes.

bombers during their bombing runs over Germany. The Germans POWS had never seen this plane; they thought that it was a German Messerschmitt (ME 109). They started shouting, clapping, and whistling until they saw the markings on the underside of the wings.

Convoy's Orders Changed

We were traveling west when our ambulance convoy received a message to continue to Casablanca instead of Oran. Therefore, a serious decision had to be made regarding my situation.

I wondered whether I should continue to Casablanca with the convoy or try to get to Oran. I knew that there was a naval base at Oran. I was not too positive about Casablanca. I opted to try for Oran. We arrived at the crossroads leading to Oran where I was deposited. This was exactly as stated, a crossroads and nothing else. I was in the middle of nowhere and at the intersection of two roads, with all of my gear and wondering what happens next? I was about fifty miles from Oran. A jeep with Navy Shore Patrol sailors (SP) saw me and picked me up. They also thought that I was AWOL. I was taken to the Naval base at Oran. There it was discovered that I was not AWOL and I had finally reached my destination of Oran.

Bizerte Bound

The Navy put me up for the night in the naval barracks. The next day arrangements were made for me to board another LST. It would take me to Lake Bizerte where my ship was docked. I boarded this LST and during the eastward trip we were side swiped by another LST A hole was knocked in our side but it was nothing serious. A metal plate was welded over the hole. We continued eastward to Lake Bizerte. There I was able to locate my ship, the LST 351.

I finally was put aboard my ship and the entire crew was happy to see me. The first thing I did after settling in my old bunk was to talk to the person responsible for the mail. He told me that he was glad to see me as he had saved all of my mail. Then he promptly informed me that it all had been sent back the day before my return. I had not

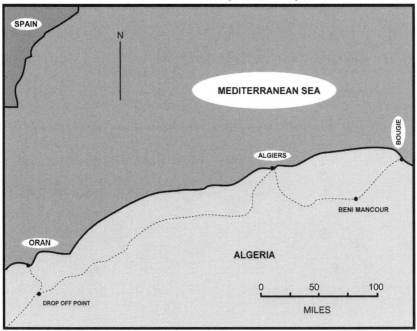

Fig 12. A detailed sketch of Bob's hectic trip across North Africa, including the drop off point south of Oran.

received any mail since we left New York (probably three months). There were two mail bags filled with my mail when it finally caught up with me. My mother was sending me the Grand Rapids Press every day. This took up most of the bulk of my mail. One of the most important things for a sailor is to receive mail from home.

Ann Lee

The sailors on our ship had very little opportunity to visit any of the shows put on by famous radio or motion picture stars. The timing just did not work to our advantage. However, there was one time in Lake Bizerte that almost our entire crew was invited to a show in a big warehouse. The featured performer was Ann Lee. She was a beautiful redhead and dressed in a skin-tight, green evening gown. Most of the men in the audience were sailors . Some of the sailors remarked that Miss Lee had been poured into her gown.

She invited one of the sailors on to the stage. She told him that

Fig 13. Two LSTs and 4 LCT's at Bizerte. Notice the 4 LCTs in the lower right corner and their relative size to the LST's.

she was to be in a movie and needed practice for her lines. She handed this sailor a script and told him to read the male lines. She would recite her lines at the proper time. Naturally, it was a love scene. The sailor began to read and Ann came very close to this sailor. There were several exchanges of the script and Ann was quite close. The sailor dropped the papers and suddenly pushed Ann away. Ann asked him what was the matter? The sailor replied, "You do not know how long I have been away from home. " The crowd roared.

Shrapnel Scratch

We were anchored in Lake Bizerte and almost every night the Germans would bomb us. The anti-aircraft guns firing at the enemy planes would project a shell or many shells at the aircraft. These shells would burst into thousands of pieces of shrapnel forming a black cloud. These black clusters are called "flak."

I was standing watch on the bridge during one of these night air raids. I was crouched down in the splinter shield. This is a semi-circular metal shield that is designed to deflect any metal fragments to protect those on the bridge. We were in port so I was the only person on duty on the bridge. A piece of shrapnel came down, hit the inside of the splinter shield, ricocheted, and cut my left hand. It was only a scratch about five inches long but there was some bleeding. The splinter shield had done its job and the piece of shrapnel was well spent when it hit my hand.

I cleaned the scratch with some gauze from the signal area first aid kit. My scout and Red Cross training indicated that I should always be prepared. I had obtained several sulfa powder packets from various army medics I had met. We were taught during our training the benefits of using sulfa powder on an open wound. I always kept some on hand. I put some sulfa powder on the cut on the back of my left hand.

The next day the pharmacist mate said it was only a scratch and that I would be all right. I still have the piece of shrapnel that cut my hand.

Clarification Of the Purple Heart Award

Sometimes, during an air raid some of the ships would be in motion. We were anchored during this air raid in which I was wounded. An LCI was passing across our bow.

A bomb hit the LCI that was quite close to our ship. We picked up many of the survivors and our pharmacist mate was very busy with the casualties from that LCI. I mentioned to him about my scratch and he looked at it during his hustle and bustle of taking care of the survivors from the LCI. Therefore, he probably was so occupied with the injured that he apparently never entered into his logbook this incident concerning the scratch on my hand.

I did not think that this injury was sufficient to warrant the Purple Heart. However, when I was ready for discharge the person interviewing me at Columbia University was asking me questions about my war experiences and specifically requested information regarding any injury. I mentioned my scratch and he said that there was no information in my records regarding any wound as a result of enemy action. He said if the injury caused any bleeding, no matter how slight, it would be sufficient to warrant earning the medal.

Fig 14. A picture of an LCI underway at sea.

The same types of questions were put forth to me at the Great Lakes Naval Training Center. It was from here that I received my final instructions for my discharge. The officer doing my final briefing made the same statement that I was entitled to the Purple Heart Medal. Any military person that is wounded during enemy action is awarded this special medal. "Wounded" is defined as drawing some blood as a result of enemy action.

I requested from the Navy (after my discharge) receipt of my medals and awards. The Navy Department sent me some of my medals. The Purple Heart was sent to me along with my other medals. I was missing some of my awards and medals and therefore requested the balance of those due to me. The Navy Department sent me a notice that they had perused my records and they could not find any record of my earning the Purple Heart. [They also instructed me to return the Purple Heart that was previously mailed to me, they are still waiting]. The information regarding the Purple Heart is written on my discharge papers. I have not received my additional medal as of February 1 1999.

The Navy has a special name for a rumor: it is "scuttlebutt." There was a scuttlebutt story that a jeep driver hit a mine which blew up his jeep and sent him flying. The soldier had many bruises but no indication of any blood. They took him to the hospital and the doctor examined him and found no signs of bleeding. The doctor scratched him with a needle and stated that the wounded soldier was now eligible for the Purple Heart.

A Slip of the Tongue

There was a woman named Gertie who broadcast by radio, propaganda for the Germans. We called her "Dirty Gertie from Bizerte." It was amazing how accurate some of her broadcasts were after each air raid. The day after the LCI next to us was hit "Dirty Gertie" broadcast the identification number of this LCI plus some information regarding the crew. The men we had recovered said this information was very accurate. Here is another true-to-life reason why you have to be very careful of what and to whom you may repeat some of the smallest of details.

Fig 15. Another view of an LCI at sea.

Salt Water and Burns Do not Mix

Several of the men we recovered from that LCI were badly burned. The burns plus exposure to the salt water caused these areas to become quite bloated. Fortunately all the men we picked up lived. These survivors were later transferred to the hospital on shore.

Strangely, those who were wearing long underwear were burned only on their hands, their feet, and their face. The others were burned over more areas of their body. My medical training came in handy again as I was able to assist in the treatment of the survivors, after I finished my watch. My primary assistance was in administering morphine and giving blood plasma to the injured.

A Transfer at Sea

There is one event that may happen at sea that many sailors never get the opportunity to witness. It is the transfer of a person from one ship to another while at sea. A light line is sent from one ship to another. There is a heavier line attached to the first line. This heavier line is connected to a set of supports and pulleys. There is a set of pulleys placed on this heavy line. An odd appearing canvas seat is fastened to the pulley. There are two light lines fastened to this chair arrangement. One line is fastened to each side of the seat system. This permits a definite directional movement of the lines from each ship. The person being transferred wears a kapok life jacket (the latest in naval design). He or she is asked to sit in the canvas chair with feet dangling. The sailors on the receiving ship pull on their line until the person is safely aboard. The rolling of the ships naturally makes the supporting line dip. The visual result may be quite humorous. Fortunately I was permitted to observe this transfer. The chair arrangement is called a "breeches buoy."

The Amphibious Fleet

The amphibious fleet is made up of several different ships and boats. The five ships are each ocean going and the boats can be carried on some of the ships. The boats are: **LCT**, Landing Craft Tanks; **LCVP**, Landing Craft Vehicle Personnel; **LCM**, Landing Craft Medium. There are several more boats in the amphibious fleet but I was unfamiliar with those. The five ocean traveling ships in increasing size are: **LCI**, Landing Craft Infantry; **LSM**, Landing Ship Medium; **LST**, Landing

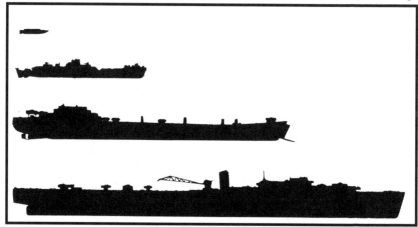

Fig 16. A silhouette size comparison of various landing crafts. Starting at the top they are:
LCVP-Landing Craft Vehicle Personnel
LCI-Landing Craft Infantry
LST-Landing Ship Tank
LSD-Landing Ship Dock

Ship Tanks; **LSD**, Landing Ship Dock; and **APA**, Attack Transport. A more detailed description and their function will be given under the functions of the amphibious navy

Plan of an Invasion

The beach to be invaded will be bombarded by the shells of the ships of the line; battleships, cruisers, and destroyers. Bombers will bomb this same area. This bombarding may go on for several days. This is referred to as the softening up process. It would appear that no one could survive this extensive bombing and shelling. History has shown us that this is not necessarily true.

The invasion time may be preceded by a group of paratroopers landing behind the enemy lines to cut communications, supply lines, or raise havoc to some installations.

A number of infantry troops will land on this shore at a designated time. These soldiers or marines will be conveyed to the beach in a number of different vehicles, this is referred to as the initial or first wave. This part of the operation was determined by the tides, amount of moonlight, and the time to daylight. Then at a later time on the same day support vehicles; tanks, half tracks, trucks, jeeps, artillery weapons, and additional personnel will be landed on the shore.

Fig 17. These 6 LCTs are being floated down the river. This model is different and smaller than other models.

Amphibious Navy Functions (Boats)

The functions and the purpose of the amphibious fleet were:

1. Bring men, supplies, and vehicles to the shores of the enemy.

2. Continue this supply of the military items to the allied forces that have previously landed. The landing craft were all flat bottom to facilitate their beach landing.

The LCTs, and LCVPs have a forward ramp that permits rapid unloading. onto the beach

There were several types of the LCTs. Sometimes used as a shuttle between the larger ships and the shore, for troops or supplies. An LCT could carry several trucks and 1 or 2 tanks. The LCT was carried on the top deck of an LST. An LCT is over 100 feet in length.

An LCVP is designed to only carry infantry troops. This boat was approximately thirty six feet long. There would be a navy or coast

Fig 18. An LCT being loaded onto the top deck of an LST. There were several different models and sizes of LCTs. An LCT could not be loaded on our 6 davit ship as the extra davits did not permit sufficient off loading of the LCT which was unloaded over the side.

guard crew of 3-5 sailors. The LCVP could carry up to 36 troops. The LCVP is hung on the LST from davits. These davits are composed of two "C" frames with a pulley and a steel cable at the top end of the "C."

The boats would be lowered to the water by means of a power winch attached to the steel cables. The troops would climb down a rope

Fig 19. The loading of soldiers into an LCVP. Other soldiers are climbing down the rope ladder into another LCVP. Note: the two machine guns mounted on the stern of the LCVP's.

Fig 20. An LCT being used as a shuttle of troops, probably from a troop ship. This LCT is different and larger than the 2 previous boats

net into this small boat. This is no easy task for the troops loaded down with their battle gear in rolling seas. The hooking and unhooking to the davit cable had to be done at the same time, otherwise one end would be suspended while the other end was in the water. This became a tricky operation and required much practice.

Fig 21. LCVPs circling and awaiting to follow the guide LCVP towards the enemy shore at the designated time "H-Hour".

One of our LCVP's would be used to ferry men to the pier if the LST was anchored in a bay or a lake. It was also used sometimes to bring supplies to the ship, if for some reason we could not approach the beach or a pier.

Fig 22. The loading of soldiers into a number of LCVPs at a dock. Note: the inflating of the barrage balloons in the background.

Twenty to thirty LCVPs could be carried by an APA (attack Transport). These LCVPs would be loaded with troops by means of a net over the side, just as they would be from an LST.

Fig 23. A picture of a loaded LCVP with 36 infantry troops. The boat crew can be identified by their white hats.

Amphibious Navy Functions (Ships)

The **LCI** (Fig 24), an ocean going vessel was designed to carry up to 200 troops. It had a 2 section ramp on either side that could be lowered to required levels. The troops would load and embark down these ramps. This group of troops is referred to as the second wave or support infantry. It would approach the shore as far as possible shortly after high tide, drop its stern anchor, lower the ramps and discharge the troops. The pull of the rear anchor and with sufficient water under the ship it would be able to back off the beach. It then assembles into a returning convoy to the base to repeat the process over again.

If the LCI was used for a cargo other than troops it had to be unloaded item by item by hand. This was a very slow and time consuming process.

The **LST** (Fig 26), another ocean going vessel was about 350 feet long, about 50 feet wide, had two huge bow doors, an internal, adjustable height ramp, and was flat bottomed similar to all of the landing craft. It was often termed a man made whale due to its wide open mouth. Sometimes called a floating tunnel.

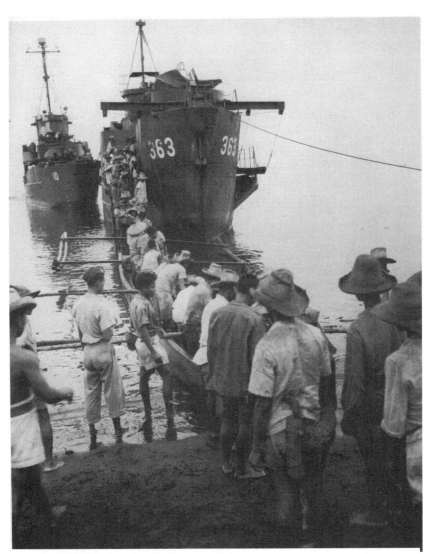

Fig 24. Another view of an LCI; note: the ramp and the
hand to hand unloading.

The LST had two decks. The top deck was connected to the
tank deck by means of a large elevator. This is the same elevator mentioned earlier in the describing the accident at the Norfolk coal dock
The main deck can carry all moving vehicles except the tanks and the
larger artillery. Normally, the ship enters the loading area with the bow
(front) straight onto the pier. The smaller vehicles, jeeps, anti-aircraft
weapons, 6x6 trucks, etc. were driven up the ramp and loaded onto the
elevator and raised to the upper deck and placed in position on the deck

and tied down. The elevator is locked into position with heavy pins. The main deck becomes a large parking lot.

Fig 25. The top deck of an LST.

The LST also had either 2 or 6 davits ("C" frames) to carry LCVPs. These LCVPs would be loaded with infantry troops and join the first wave invasion group. An LST would approach the enemy shore, after the return of the LCVPs. This approach must take place shortly after high tide. The stern anchor is dropped and the LST goes toward the beach as far as it is possible.

Fig 26. A six (6) davit LST capable of carrying six LCVPs.

Fig 27. The loading of an LST, again illustrating its versatility, this time it is a field kitchen.

Fig 28. The loading of trucks and anti-aircraft weapons aboard LSTs. These vehicles will be placed on the top deck.

The bow of the LST would be on dry land if the angle of the beach was favorable and there were no sand bars. Many times this was not feasible. Ofttimes the vehicles left the ramp in the water. The tanks would drive straight out then followed by those vehicles which were on the top deck. The LST then had to wait until the next tide. The tank deck would be loaded with prisoners or causalities for the return trip. The ramp and the open bow doors facilitated the loading of the wounded as an ambulance could drive right up into the tank deck.

The high tide and the pull of the stern anchor would permit the LST to back off the beach. It would anchor off shore and wait until a convoy could be formed The LST would continue these trips as long as necessary. An LST had a crew of 90 to 110 men, and 9 to 11 officers. It was powered by two diesel engines with twin screws.

Fig 29. A Sherman tank leaving an LST. This photo illustrates the prime function of an LST.

The next step is the loading of the tanks. The medium Sherman tanks would then be backed onto the tank deck, three abreast. An LST can carry 30 Sherman tanks. There was very little room between the tanks. The ramp is pulled up and the bow doors shut and locked. The loading of the mobile cargo was now completed.

An **LSD** (figure 30) was a floating dry dock. It was capable of repairing all types of amphibious craft. This ship was over 400 feet long. The LSD could also carry several LCVPs that could be launched off the open stern.

Fig-30. A Photo of an LSD, (Landing Ship Dock.)

Fig 31. A number of troops leaving LSTs after the ships have beached.

An **APA** is an ocean going vessel that may have been converted from a merchant ship. It could carry 20-30 LCVPs, some on davits, others on the deck. The APA was not flat bottomed so it could not approach the beach. The unloading of the additional supplies had to be loaded onto an LCT or other means of transferring items to the beach. The APAs were considerably larger than the LSTs, therefore, could carry more cargo and troops. The movie "Away All Boats" is an excellent representation of the APAs.

Pontoons

Many times the slope of the beach prevented the LSTs reaching dry land and the debarking vehicles had to traverse through water. A system was devised to alleviate this condition. Some LSTs carried a pontoon that was fastened to both sides of the ship. These pontoons were approximately 70 feet long, 10 feet wide, made of steel, and able to support the weight of several Sherman tanks at one time. There could be an additional approach of 140 feet with this system. The following photograph illustrate this condition (Fig 32).

Unscheduled Inoculations

Our crew all received a series of shots. Normally this is not unusual as there was a regular schedule for our shots. However, we received a series of shots that were not according to the normal schedule. Therefore, we knew that we were headed for some enemy war action.

Fig 32. This LST has 2-70 foot pontoon sections extending from the bow to aid in the unloading. The vehicles can now approach the beach in relative dryness. Note the pontoon extension ramp.

Fig 33. Another illustration of the utilization of pontoons. Combined they produce a ramp of over 125 feet.

Fig 34. This LST is unloading a bulldozer and other mobile units by means of pontoons. This same LST was later converted to a carrier of railroad cars that were transferred to the French rail system at Cherbourg.
Note: the barrage balloons.

We knew that all of our training was going to be put to an actual test.

"H-Hour" and "D-Day"

The use of shortcuts has led to many acronyms. The Navy was no exception. The exact hour the invasion force is to land on the enemy shore was referred to "H-Hour." Every invasion had its specific "H-Hour." The day on which an invasion takes place is called "D-Day." Every invasion also had its specific "D-Day." Our first "H-Hour" and "D-Day" was code named **"Husky"**.

The most famous of these "D-Day" invasions was the day the Allies invaded France at Normandy, June 6, 1944.

The first wave of troops was expected to land at "H-Hour" on "D-Day." Rough seas, loss of sight of the leading LCVP, fog, and collisions, were some of the reasons that this was not always possible.

The first wave of troops would be loaded into LCVP's form LSTs and APAs. Each LCVP carried thirty-six (36) troops. Our ship the LST 351 had six LCVPs. The APAs carried twenty to thirty LCVPs. Each LCVP had a crew of three or four navy or coast guard persons.

These LCVPs circled at a designated area until all the LCVPs were ready for landing. This group of landing craft was one of many that would be the initial invasion force to land on an enemy beach. At the proper time, these boats began heading towards shore. This was the initiation of "H-Hour".

Fig 35. Soldiers assisting in the discharge of a Jeep from an LST. The ramp is almost on dry land. It is possible that the Jeep stalled from the engine becoming wet during the unloading. This could have been avoided if pontoons were available for this landing. Notice the man on top of these huge doors.

Invasion Preparation

We loaded our tank deck with Sherman tanks after we had already brought half tracks and many trucks for an artillery unit up to our main deck.

We also had on board 216 men who would be part of the first wave of troops that would be asked to land on some foreign beach. We carried six LCVP's. These boats are often referred to as "Higgins Boats." A Mr. Andrew Higgins of New Orleans designed and produced these landing craft. Each of these boats would be lowered from davits and would hold thirty-six, first-wave invasion, infantry troops.

These first wave troops would shoulder the brunt of the invasion. Most of the soldiers on our ship had never been exposed to real action and many of them were 18, 19, and 20 years old. I had not yet reached my 21st birthday

Day before the Invasion

Fig 36. A picture of LSTs with barrage balloons.
note: the gaping bow doors.

We were crossing the Mediterranean Sea. There was a British battleship ahead of us in the convoy. It was the day before our scheduled landing, July 8, 1943. It was the middle of the afternoon and the weather was clear. There was a German fighter plane that flew over the convoy. It was a German Folke Wulf 190 (FW 190) fighter plane.

This plane came at the convoy out of the sun; and it was

difficult to see the plane. The pilot started to strafe (this is the term for a plane to fire its machine guns at the convoy). This plane also dropped some of its bombs at the ships behind us. There was a barrage balloon tied to our ship.

This barrage balloon had a steel cable tied to it but otherwise is free flying. It is filled with helium and is used on the beach to prevent low flying airplanes from attacking the troops. If that German pilot had run into our balloon, it would have sliced his wing in two. The pilot could see this so he began to bank to the right. I was on the bridge and jumped over the railing and went to the wing where there was a machine gun. I pulled the bolt back to put a shell in the chamber and started to lead the German plane as I was taught in gunnery school. The pilot was close enough that I could see the expression on his face.

I wondered if I could hit this plane. I was concentrating on the lessons given at gunnery school. If I hit the FW 190 would it crash? What would happen to the pilot? Would he be picked up by some allied ship ? All of these thoughts were running through my mind while I was waiting for an officer to give me the order to fire. The officers on the bridge did not give the order to fire. They were dumbfounded (I guess). Therefore, this German pilot was permitted to get away and warn the German troops that a large convoy was approaching Italy. Navy regulations state that a gun may not be fired until a direct firing order is spoken. The British battleship in front of us was unable to fire for fear of hitting someone on our ship.

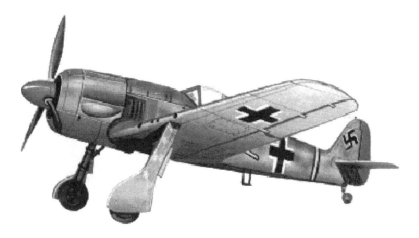

Fig 37. A German fighter plane, FW 190. This is the type of plane that spotted our convoy the day before the Sicily invasion.

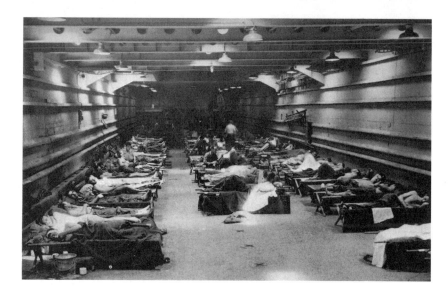

Fig 38. The tank deck of an LST. This photo illustrates this area being utilized as a hospital area for the wounded on a return trip.

Fig 39. A Sherman tank debarking from the gaping mouth of an LST. 30 of these can fit into the tank deck of the LST above.

Purpose of Six LCVP's

Our particular LST had an additional function. We carried six LCVPs (**L**anding **C**raft **V**ehicle **P**ersonnel), as mentioned earlier. Each LCVP can carry thirty-six infantry troops. These infantry troops would be the first persons to go ashore for an invasion. Some of the other LSTs had only two LCVPs. These LCVPs are mounted on davits with a steel cable at each end. These boats would be lowered and the infantry troops would be loaded, then circle with other LCVPs at a designated

Fig 40. A loaded LCVP headed for the invasion beach.

position. They would approach the beach and arrive there at the appointed hour. This hour was given the acronym of "H-Hour." The LCVP was also flat bottomed and had a ramp at the front. The LCVP would land on the shore and lower its ramp. The infantry troops would then disembark. There were occasions that the boat would hit a sand bar. Then the departing soldiers found themselves in the water over their heads.

Fig 41. The loading of 2 LSTs from the dock. This is the view that resembled a whale's mouth.

Importance of the Tide

Normally, the ship will approach the shore at some time after high tide. Then at the next high tide there would be sufficient water under the ship to permit the ship to float. The combination of tide and the pulling of the stern anchor would bring the ship into a position of self movement

Fig 42. An aerial view of several LSTs on the beach. A bulldozer has moved sand to permit the vehicles to embark onto dry land. This can be only accomplished where there is a shallow tide.

While the LST would wait for high tide, it would take on cargo for the return trip. This human cargo of prisoners or wounded personnel would be transported back to the originating base. The LST would lie at anchor with other ships until a convoy could be assembled. The convoy would return to a base and the LSTs would unload their cargo. These ships would load up again and make the crossing with more materiel for the invading forces.

Storm and Seasick Soldiers

One of our LCVP boats broke loose from the davit during the storm. I was part of a maintenance group that was to try to anchor it down as well as to determine if it was still functional. I went to the bow and had a line that I was trying to loop around part of the LCVP to anchor it. The banging of this small boat created much noise and possibly was causing some damage I was standing on the ammunition box, leaning against the ramp of the small boat while trying to cast the loop. We had to get a line around the LCVP to assist us in tying it to the davit. There was a sudden lurch and then there was nothing between the Mediterranean Sea and myself. Fortunately, someone held onto my belt

Fig 43. Unloading a truck and trailer from the top deck, note the elevator opening from the top deck directly under the ship's number 579.

Fig 44. A truck leaving the bow of an LST. This picture illustrates the size of the bow door opening and the versatility of this craft.

to keep me from falling into the sea.

We finally were able to secure this LCVP but testing the davit we realized that it would not function the next day. This meant that the thirty-six soldiers who would normally go in this boat would have to be distributed among the other five boats.

Fig 45. A photo of an LST's front end showing the ramp and the bow door.

Operation "Husky"

Our destination was to be Licata, Sicily. The code name for this operation was "Husky." All operations have a code name. The soldiers on board were extremely sea sick. It was estimated that over seventy percent of these young men were sick and very weak. "H-Hour" was scheduled to occur at 0245 on July 10, 1943. It was less than 13 months from the time I started "boot camp" until I was involved with my first invasion. It was soon approaching the time for us to anchor and await for the proper hour to lower our boats. This hour was referred to as "H-Hour". The evening before the invasion we encountered a terrible storm, and most of the soldiers were sea sick. Most of our invasion soldiers had not seen any enemy action. It is difficult enough for inexperienced soldiers to make a landing on enemy soil without adding seasickness to their problems. The mental and the physical condition of these soldiers left much to be desired.

Unheeded Warning

A control ship traveled alongside our LST and informed us that it was time to drop our anchor. Our captain who had been in the Merchant Marine for many years was drunk He had requisitioned the liquor from sick bay. He cussed and swore at the man on the control ship. We kept going closer to the shore. The control ship again warned us that we were in too far and to drop anchor. Our captain kept going and going. We finally dropped our bow anchor. We were considerably

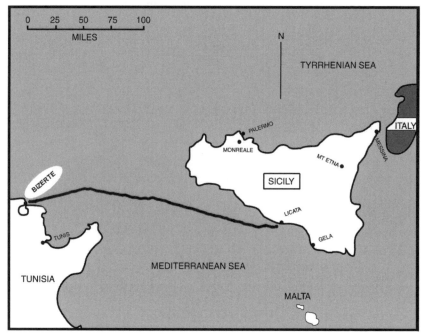

Fig 46. A map showing relative distances from Sicily to North African ports. The invasion fleet from Tunis and Bizerte sailed in an easterly direction towards Sicily (line).

closer to the beach than the required four miles. We tested the winch for the forward anchor and realized that it was inoperable as a result of the storm. This meant that when we were ready to move from our anchorage the steel cable connected to the anchor would have to be cut. The steel cable, approximately two inches in diameter, for this anchor would have to be cut with an acetylene torch.

An Oversize Cigar

We were at anchor off the landing area at Licata and awaiting for "H-hour" when a bright light appeared on the bridge. It was our captain smoking a cigar. I swear that cigar looked to be ten inches in diameter. This bright circle of light could compromise our position to the enemy. There was a young soldier on the bow next to me. This soldier was one of the young men who had been seasick He saw that light from the cigar He took his carbine off his shoulder, took a clip from his belt and inserted it into the rifle He then loaded a shell in the chamber and rested the rifle on something to support it and lined up on that cigar. I pleaded with him not to pull the trigger and told him that he would be ruining his life if he pulled the trigger. There were several long anxious minutes before he lowered his gun and took out the clip. Shortly thereafter the captain went below. Remember the soldiers were sea sick and the information about the damaged small boat did not help matters.

"Friendly Fire"

Another event that occurred while we were waiting was the shooting down of some of our C-47 planes carrying paratroopers. The shooting was being done by our ships. I was in position to observe the actual firing by our troops on these C-47 planes. We could see some of the planes go down after being shot. This is what is meant by the expression "shot down by friendly fire."

The events of the previous evening created a tension among some of our ships and many of the men were very edgy.

German 88 mm Battery

We were anxiously awaiting the dawn to see how far we were off the beach. We were supposed to be about four miles from the shore. The sky became lighter and brighter and a German battery of three 88 mm, (slightly larger than three inches), cannons spotted us and began firing at our ship . This was the result of our captain not following the orders of the control ship.

The Germans fired at us in clusters of three shells (probably one battery). We were only three quarters of a mile from the beach. The first three shells hit about one-hundred feet off our port bow; the next three hit off our starboard side. The officer on the bridge gave the order to cut the anchor cable and get us out of there. We were ready with the acetylene torch and began cutting the steel cable immediately. This took

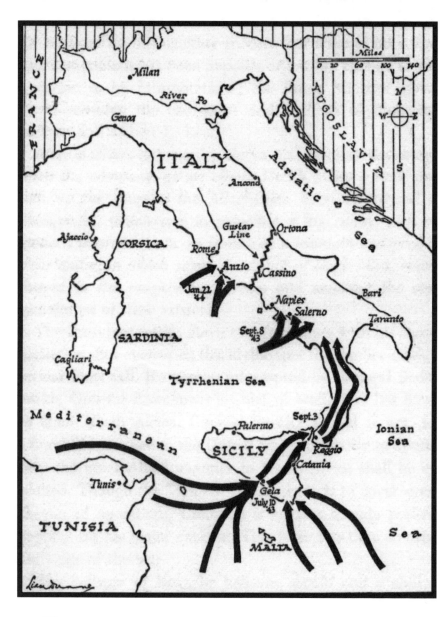

Fig 47. From Tunisia, the allies cross to Sicily on July 10,
1943, to open the Italian Campaign.
On September 3, Allied armies secure a foothold
at Reggio and link with forces landed at Salerno
on September 8. At Cassino, the German Gustav
Line in the mountains is almost impregnable. On
January 22, 1944, the Allies gain a bloody
beachhead at Anzio, and on two fronts, German

a few seconds. (The anchor was replaced on our return trip to Bizerte.) The strain on the steel cable caused us to be pulled to port. The next three shells landed exactly in that location from which we had just moved. The exploding shells created shrapnel fragments that landed on our deck. (I later gathered some of the shrapnel fragments and still have them today). Fortunately no one was injured by these fragments. We pulled back to the four miles where we should have been originally

Fig 48. A picture of a Sherman tank traversing a pile of rubble. The angle of the armor below the canon was an identifying feature as explained to us by the tank men.

after we cut the anchor cable. Here we had to wait for high tide as the LST is designed to go as fast as it can towards the beach shortly after high tide. This water under the ship plus the pulling by the stern anchor permits the LST to back off the beach. An LST only draws about twelve feet when loaded (probably only nine feet at the bow).

Demise of German Tanks

My duties were such that I was to stay on the bow and relay phone messages from the bridge to the officer at the bow. It was very dark and practically no moon but we could just see the silhouette of a small hill. We could see a German "Tiger" tank approach this hill.

Suddenly, there was a blast from one of the cruisers behind us The cruiser had fired two shells from its six inch guns. The German tank that we could see in silhouette was blown to bits. Then there was another tank, another blast, and scratch another tank. This happened three times before the Germans decided to go around this hill instead of over it. We think the cruiser that was doing the firing was either the *Brooklyn* or the *Philadelphia*. Their spotting of the enemy, their gun control , and the subsequent accuracy was phenomenal. A comparison of Sherman and Panzer tanks follows:

British Supplies for American Sailors

On one of the trips we stopped at the island of Malta but no shore leave was given to any of the men. There was one period when we were sailing in and out of Tunisia that we received British supplies: horse meat in lieu of steaks, (it tasted very good), and SOS (chipped beef on toast), we sailors called it "Shit On a Shingle." We had this every other day for breakfast for about six weeks. The other days we had pancakes made with powdered milk and powdered eggs. We had a cook on board who did everything to doctor up the powdered milk to make it more palatable. The milk would taste like chalk if it were not mixed with vanilla or some other spice.

Fig 49. Silhouettes of two German Panzer tanks with the American Sherman medium sized tank (bottom). The German Mark IV is on the top and the Mark III is in the center.

British Air Cover

We were waiting for the proper time to beach and discharge our moving cargo tanks, trucks, jeeps, etc. There were two British Spitfire airplanes circling overhead and everyone thought that it was part of our allied air cover

However, the higher ups forgot that there were not to be any British airplanes in this sector. The two Spitfires had earlier been captured by the Germans who were using them against the Allies. The anti-aircraft gunners, not knowing this, began to relax. The Spitfires then dive bombed and strafed the ships that were anchored or on the beach. These two Spitfires ultimately left the invasion area. We pulled off the beach at the proper time with the help of the high tide and the pull of the stern anchor. A convoy was formed and we sailed for North Africa.

Fig 50. A British fighter plane, Spitfire.

Fig 51. A German fighter plane, ME-109.

U-Boat Commander Miscalculates

Most of our trips back and forth to Sicily began from Lake Bizerte, Algeria (North Africa). It was during one of these return trips that another unusual event happened. We were in the Mediterranean not too far from Bizerte and traveling empty. A submerged German submarine spotted us and fired a torpedo directly at us. The commander of this submarine did not realize how shallow our draft was and probably set the torpedo depth at approximately fifteen feet. I happened to be standing on the port side when I saw the wake of the torpedo as it was headed right for us. We were only drawing about nine feet so the torpedo sailed right under us. (The draft is the depth of the ship in the water). This was by far the my most frightening moment of the war.

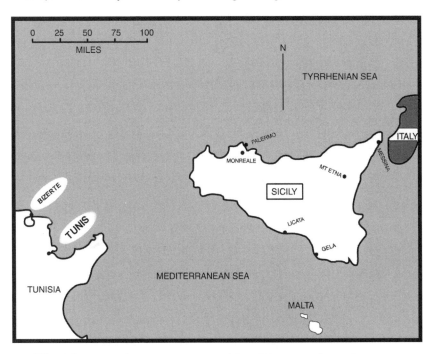

Fig 52. Our ship was approaching Bizerte when the U-Boat captain fired a torpedo.

Cities of Sicily

Sometimes our trips would take us to Palermo, the capital city of the island province of Sicily. Monreale was close to Palermo. I was on liberty and visited this city on one of our stops. I was really impressed by the mosaic art in the cathedral at Monreale. Many Bible stories were depicted on the walls of the cathedral of Monreale. This was my first encounter with mosaic art.

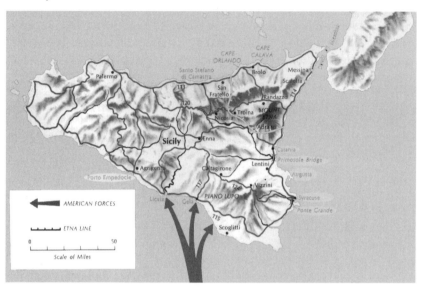

Fig 53. The map of Sicily and the toe of Italy. The initial landings were at Licata and Gela.

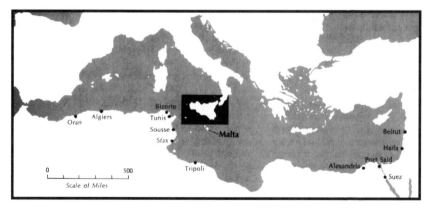

Fig 54. The island of Sicily is indicated in the highlighted inset.

Fast Flags

We sailed several times to the port of Taranto. This was after the invasion of Salerno. Taranto is the big Italian naval base located in the southern part of Italy. If you look at a map of Italy you would see that it is the shape of a boot. It is located at the top of the heel of this boot. It was during one of these stops that I happened to be the signalman on duty as we were coming in to the harbor Sometimes we would receive docking orders by radio, sometimes by Morse code sent by a big sixteen inch light. This particular day there was a man standing

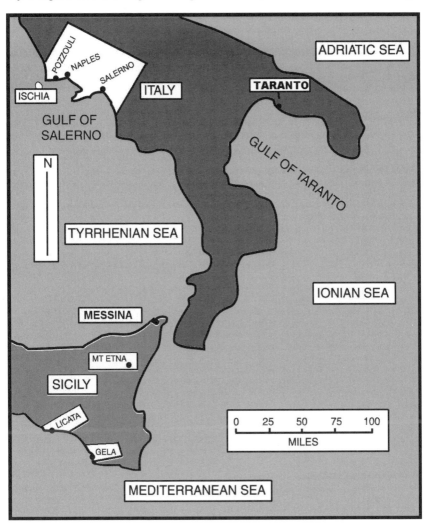

Fig 55. Sketch showing Taranto, Salerno and Naples. Pozzouli and Ischia are also shown.

on top of a building that was several stories tall and he was sending our docking orders by semaphore. All that could be seen of this Italian sailor was his silhouette against the sky. I believe that he was several miles away. I was later told that his rate of sending this message was about thirty words a minute. This is exceptionally fast for semaphore. The normal speed is twelve to twenty words per minute.

Changing Light Bulbs

A ship is much like a home. There are some regular maintenance items that must be done. However, some of these chores involved a little more of a hazard than you would meet at home. One of these was the changing of burnt out light bulbs. These particular bulbs were part of our identification system and had to be in working order at all times. These lights were up on the mast and somewhat difficult to change. You had to stand on a mast stay (a steel cable suspended under the yard arm), and then you had to hang or hold on to the yard arm with one hand and change the light bulb with the other hand. You first had to unhook the colored glass, then unscrew the bulb, and replace it with the good bulb. All of this time the cable under your feet was swaying back and forth.

Fig 56. A picture of an LST at sea. This particular LST was converted to a hospital LST. It was later part of the A-Bomb test at the Bikini Atoll.

We usually changed these bulbs while we were in port because the ship would have less tendency to sway. However, there was one time at sea that one of our lights burned out and had to be replaced. This particular day the sea was a little rough. The importance of these colored lights required that the bulb be changed immediately.

Therefore, I had to climb the mast to change the bulb. The rocking and the rolling of the ship made this chore very dangerous. The task was completed but I sure was happy to put my feet on the solid deck. Fortunately, this event only happened one time for me.

"Cat Fever" or Malaria

There were several times that I was not feeling very well and I would be running a fever. The pharmacist mate said it was "cat fever." Later I learned that this was short for catarrh fever. This was a semi-technical term for a fever of unknown cause.

The entire crew had been ordered to take atabrine tablets to prevent malaria on a regular basis since the first day we had landed at Oran. These atabrine tablets caused a yellowish tinge to the skin.

Later during my attendance at Loyola University in Chicago in 1946 I was not feeling very well. The school doctor at Loyola University suggested that I go to the Veterans Hospital in Chicago. The doctors performed several tests and determined that I had malaria. The doctors at the hospital determined that I had the 25 year version of this disease. This meant that if I did not drink and took care of myself the malaria would run its course within 25 years. I probably contracted this disease while I was in the British Field Hospital at Bougie. Malaria is the result of being bitten by a disease carrying mosquito. I was bitten many times by mosquitoes while I was in the hospital at Bougie, Algeria. If I contacted this while in the British hospital in 1943 and my last known attack occurred in 1968 the doctors were very prophetic.

The normal cycle for a malaria attack is 28 to 30 days. There was one time, while I was attending the University of Detroit in 1948, that I had 27 attacks over a 9 month period. The doctor stated that this was a very severe situation.

A Ship's Private Transportation

It was after one of our frequent trips across the Mediterranean Sea that we did some moonlight requisitioning at Bizerte. This is the term used by sailors to obtain something without a requisition. We discovered an Army jeep that did not seem to have a driver The jeep was parked in a remote area. We took it on board the ship and painted it navy gray over the army olive green and altered the serial numbers. This became our shore transportation for a long time. We took turns using it with the officers.

However, one day when it was the enlisted men's turn to use the jeep, one of the officers while on liberty decided to use his authority and took it into town (Tunis) the capital of Tunisia. Some of the enlisted men from our ship spotted the jeep and decided to take revenge upon the officer. They made four wooden blocks with a half round surface on the top, the half-round was large enough to fit the wheels. They gathered enough men to lift the jeep onto the blocks. It was high enough that if anyone tried to take it down it could be badly damaged.

The officer called the local police and said that the jeep belonged to our ship That was the end of our on-shore transportation. Somehow the Shore Patrol recognized that the jeep was not ours and confiscated it.

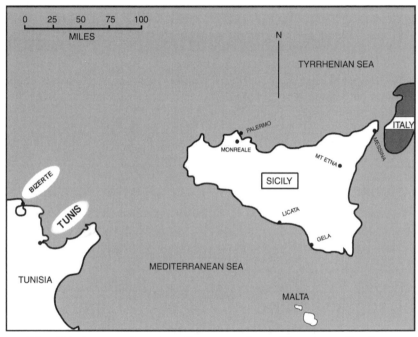

Fig 57. A map showing distances from Bizerte to Tunis.

Officers Authority

Another example of officers displaying their authority was on a day we were receiving supplies. We received a box with ten pounds of good butter (not the tropical type). This was a very unexpected but pleasant treat. The officer on duty when this box arrived had nine pounds sent to the officers' mess and the one pound was left for the enlisted men. There were nine officers on our ship and ninety enlisted men. That made nine pounds for nine officers and one pound for ninety enlisted men. This was the same officer who used his authority to take the jeep. We felt that this was an injustice.

The next time we took on supplies at Bizerte; there was a treat in store for our ship. While we were receiving several cases of sliced canned peaches, we distracted the officer in charge and we diverted the peaches into locations that the officers were not apt to look. This included the engine room, the flag locker, the first aid room, and many other locations. Then none of the officers benefited from this luxury.

A Sailor's Off Duty Relaxation

The crew did not have much time to relax but our tank deck was big enough so we could play basketball. We also played much Ping-Pong. Both of these were difficult to do in rough seas.

A sailor would be on duty for four hours unless it was "dog watch." Other times we would perform functions that were related to the running of the ship such as painting, scraping rust (these two work functions were performed many times), or whatever the officers and/or chief petty officers could think up for us to do. We had to make time to study the Blue Jackets Manual, to wash our clothes, write letters, sleep, and practice our plane identification.

Washing Clothes

There was one chore that most sailors despised: that was washing clothes. We did have a washing machine on board. However, if you could find the time to do your washing there was usually someone using the washer. Many times the washing machine did not function. Then we would take the old wash board out and do our laundry. We even attempted to tie our clothes onto a line and let the wash of the propellers clean our clothes. This system worked rather well but it caused the clothes to wear out and fray quickly.

An American Soldier with a Pet Monkey

My brother Tom was inducted into the US Army and stationed in Accra: Ghana, Africa. Tom, had a rhesus monkey for a pet; he wrote to me about the antics of his pet. The two of us corresponded with each other but were unable to meet again until the completion of the war.

Fire School

I had an experience in fire-fighting that I will never forget. This occurred in North Africa as part of our continuing program of training. I was selected as the person from our ship to take a special hands-on course in fire fighting. This was a one-day lesson. I was sent to this particular school and we learned about the different types of fires that could be encountered on board a ship. The different chemicals and methods that could be used in extinguishing the fires were also explained and demonstrated. We were asked to participate in the demonstrations.

There are three items that are necessary for any fire to continue to burn: 1-Heat; 2-Oxygen (air is 22% oxygen); and 3-Fuel. The fuel is usually the item that is burning. If any one of the three items can be eliminated then the fire will cease to burn.

There was a large open oil tank fire that was used for one of the demonstrations. We were instructed to extinguish this oil fire with chemical foam.

The last item on the agenda was to put out a gasoline fire in a simulated closed stateroom. This type of fire in confined quarters could be extremely dangerous. The instructors demonstrated to us that the best technique to extinguish this type of fire was with steam. This procedure involved two men using high pressure hoses producing an extremely fine spray. The combination of the fine spray and the heat of the fire produces steam, which would cut off the oxygen supply to the fire.

Gasoline and a limited amount of air become an extremely explosive combination. The danger was properly impressed upon us "inexperienced fire fighters." The two instructors demonstrated the proper procedure to extinguish a fire of this nature The employment of two persons was very vital. The first person would be responsible for entering the room The first person was to enter the room with the spray; he would be the man to actually put out the fire. The second sailor's function was to protect the first man with the spray nozzle held high. This fine spray would also offer some cooling to the fire and protect the first man entering the room. We were shown exactly how to do this.

I volunteered to be the number one. I entered the room with my spray nozzle held high as I was instructed. There was a sudden flash; at the time the gasoline was ignited, my number two man was startled from the flash and he jumped back. This left me unprotected. The instructor immediately grabbed the spray and began spraying my head. I was burned slightly, but the quick action of the instructor saved me from any serious burns. This amply demonstrated the need for the two-man teams. The instructor encouraged me to try again so that I would not develop a fear of this procedure. The instructor was my second man and everything went as properly planned.

A Floating Mine

One day while we were heading east in the Mediterranean, we passed a floating mine that probably had broken loose from its mooring. The many fingers protruding from this mine indicated it was a contact type. It would blow up upon contact with a ship. Our lookout spotted it and we were able to avoid it. Shortly thereafter, a British aircraft carrier was headed west. I was the signalman on duty and tried to warn the carrier about this mine. They simply ignored me at first and would not acknowledge my signals. It seems that we were just "small potatoes" to them We had to look up as the carrier passed. It sure was huge.

I then decided to send the whole message without acknowledgment and hoped that someone would read it. I kept sending the message "Urgent! Urgent! Mine in your path" over and over again. Finally the carrier acknowledged my message. As we looked astern we saw that the carrier had been able to explode the mine without any damage to their ship. We guessed it may have been a sharpshooter who was able to explode the mine.

You can get some idea of the explosive force of these mines by the amount of water that is shot up as it explodes. The mines in Normandy were considerably more powerful than those in the Mediterranean, as we were to learn.

"Avalanche"

We had made several trips back and forth between North Africa and Sicily when we received another series of injections that were not part of the normal schedule. We said, "Here we go again" and wondered where the next invasion would take place. This time it was Salerno, Italy on September 8, 1943. **"Avalanche"** was the code name for the landing at Salerno. "H-Hour" was scheduled for 0300-0400, depending upon the portion of the landing area. This city is south of Naples on the west coast of Italy. The landing was conducted on the beaches south of Salerno. The area of the battle was a broad, wide open cove.

The waterway here is called the Tyrrhenian Sea. Our part of the landing went very well. The initial invasion by the soldiers was called a complete success. Later, we heard that the Germans hid by burying themselves including some of their tanks. They hid under the sand, under haystacks, in buildings, and any other place where the invasion forces could not see them. The Germans then let the invasion forces pass over or by them. They then came out of hiding and began to cut off the troops from their supplies on the beach. (This may have been only a rumor. I guess we will never know the whole truth). This information was garnered from the wounded soldiers that returned on our ship to our latest base.

We had a little trouble getting off the beach after we had discharged our moving cargo but we finally made it. It seems that we

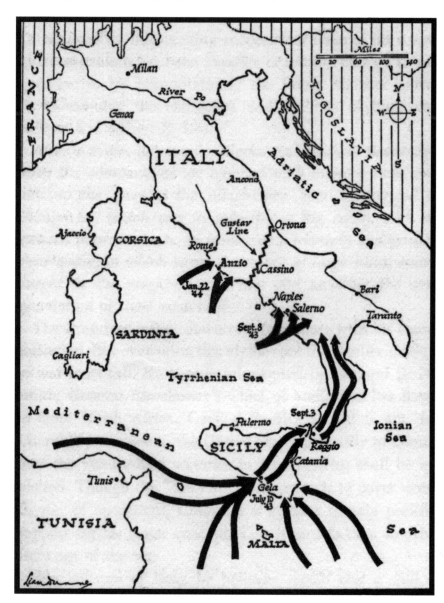

Fig 58. Map of the three landing beaches in Italy

were too far onto the beach or we may have been on a sand bar. We were able to clear the beach by moving a little forward then back. It took several attempts but we moved off and floated clear. We still had to make our trips back and forth to North Africa so it was longer between trips than when we landed in Sicily. This meant that the supply line to our troops was considerably longer.

Mementos

Our function on the return trip to North Africa was to carry prisoners or casualties. Sometimes we would transport both. I acquired a leather belt from one of the German prisoners that we took back to North Africa from Salerno. I still have this belt. The engraving on the belt is "GOTT MIT UNS" that translates into "God Be with Us." I thought that this was rather unusual considering the nature of the German attitude toward religion. I also acquired an Italian Beretta (7.65 mm automatic) with about twenty rounds of ammunition. This would be comparable to a .30 caliber bullet. It was only fired twice to make sure it was operating satisfactorily I made a canvas holster for this gun and carried it always except while on liberty and when I was sleeping. I kept it under my mattress while I was sleeping. I could not take it into the shower with me either. Our showers were salt water. The salt residue never seemed to be completely rinsed off our bodies.

I took an old bayonet and cut it down to make a sheath knife. I also made the sheath for the knife. The handle was made from a series of leather rings. I have had that knife for over fifty years. The knife and the automatic were always with me. The knife is still in my possession but the sheath has worn out. I later gave the automatic to my uncle Joe.

Life Belts Create Humorous Situations

We were ordered to constantly wear a life belt. This was a rubberized belt about five inches wide containing two tube-like compartments. The belt contained two cylinders of compressed gas, probably carbon dioxide. Squeezing on the connection of the two ends of the belt caused two needles to puncture the cylinders of compressed gas. The gas filled the two tubes and we had a belt life saver. On some occasions the gas would be released accidentally, e.g., bumping into something. This often created some embarrassing situations especially if we were on the way to our position for general quarters

Liberty in North Africa

I was able to locate a place in Bizerte that rented horses to ride. I went horse back riding several times while I was in North Africa. It was a joy to ride the Arabian horses. Arabs sure know how to breed horses. They also know how to take care of their horses. There was a time that I wished to go horse back riding but there were no horses available at the time. The man in charge of the animals showed me a camel and his motions indicated that he wanted me to ride the camel. He demonstrated to me how I was to mount this beast of the desert. I rode the camel for about one half hour. This was about half of my normal riding time. One half hour was plenty. I do not think that I was able to sit down for a week. The fellows aboard ship sure had a good laugh with me. They informed me that there would be considerably less pain if I would go drinking with them. There were members of the crew that were always thinking of getting me drunk.

A Camera for Sale

There was an American soldier that came aboard our ship in Bizerte. Soldiers would often come aboard our ship while we were in port, either to visit a friend, or trade mementos, or have some Navy chow (the Navy word for food) or buy some chocolate or cigarettes. This soldier had a wooden case containing a Leitz camera with several lens and filters. This soldier was asking twenty-five dollars for the entire box. I did not have the twenty-five dollars; I doubt that I would have been permitted to have that camera even if I had had the money. We were not permitted to have a camera on board for security reasons. That camera and case changed hands six or seven times. The last time I saw it sold it brought more than two-hundred dollars. This camera and the various lenses and filters were probably worth five hundred dollars or more.

Dented Helmets

There were two different size helmets that I had to use, depending upon my particular functions at the time. One was my normal steel helmet with a plastic liner. The other one was an oversize helmet that would fit over a set of headphones. One of my duties involved communications using the headphones. Both of these helmets had been dented from shrapnel at various times. This indicates how close I came to being hit with shrapnel. I scratched on the liner of my regular helmet all of the names of all the places that I visited.

Fooling the Censor

I wrote in one of my letters home after the invasion of Salerno that the butter cookies I had for dessert were very good. The censor did not know that in Grand Rapids there was a brand of butter cookies named Salerno. This was my method of trying to let the folks back home know in what action I was partaking. The sailors were constantly trying to let the home folks know where they had visited or seen action. This particular letter passed the censor.

The family also knew that I had a very good memory and was surprised that I kept mentioning ages and birth dates that were not correct. They did not realize that it was part of a code. There was no Grand Rapids Tribune, we did not own Revere stock, and we did not know anyone by the name of Jackie.

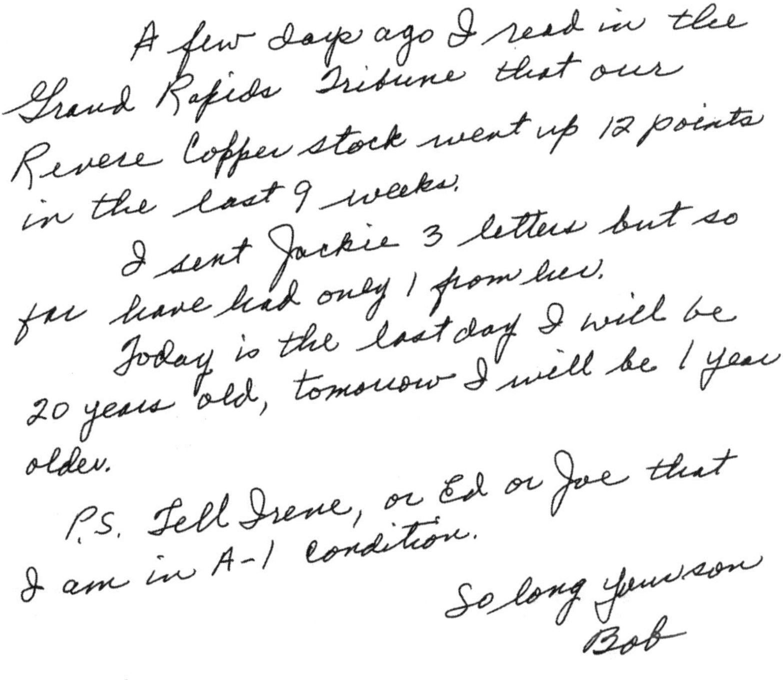

A few days ago I read in the Grand Rapids Tribune that our Revere copper stock went up 12 points in the last 9 weeks.

I sent Jackie 3 letters but so far have had only 1 from her.

Today is the last day I will be 20 years old, tomorrow I will be 1 year older.

P.S. Tell Irene, or Ed or Joe that I am in A-1 condition.

So long your son
Bob

Fig 59. A portion of the letter that was sent to the author's mother but decoded by Uncle Charlie. The numbers mentioned were a code to indicate Licata, Sicily.
[12=L; 9=I; 3=C; 1=A; 20=T]

The actual letter states "A few days ago I read in the Grand Rapids Tribune that our Revere Copper stock went up 12 points in the last 9 weeks. I sent Jackie 3 letters but so far have had only 1 from her. Today is the last day I will be 20 years old, tomorrow I will be 1 year older.

PS Tell Irene, or Ed or Joe that I am in A-1 condition"

So Long Your Son,
Bob

All the relatives saved my letters. I wrote in one of my letters that I was in A-1 condition and it would B-2 bad if the bombers were not ours. My code was 1=a, 2=b, etc. My uncle Charlie began to think about all the incorrect numbers I had included in my letters. Then he realized that I was trying to send a message. He finally interpreted the code I was trying to send. My uncle gathered all the letters I had written and he knew where I had seen action and what ports I had visited. The relatives all looked forward to decoding the letters they received.

More Mementos

I was able to obtain a portion of silk from an American parachute. I made a scarf from this silk and sent it to my uncle Ed.

We could buy a package of cigarettes for five cents. I bought a pack and tried two cigarettes and did not like them. It was the only time in my life that I tried smoking.

I sent to my mother most of my monthly pay; therefore, I had very little spending money. I would occasionally buy a chocolate bar. I would gather whatever I could in the way of canned foods or candy that I purchased from the PX (post exchange) or was able to obtain from the ship's supplies through the cook. The cook had the bunk above mine. He and I became very good friends. I would bring or give these goodies to the orphanage or to the children I would meet on the street.

Italian Churches

I had been an altar boy at St. Andrew's church in Grand Rapids while I was attending elementary school as a child. It was this early training that permitted me to assist many priests in the celebration of Holy Mass during the war. Mass was celebrated in many unusual places; it could take place in a warehouse, or aboard ship, or sometimes in an open field. This happened while I was a patient in the British field hospital.

I was assisting a priest at Mass in an Italian church and the priest used a very tiny cup that was fastened to a chain. This cup was used to dip the water and then add to the wine. Normally the priest will pour a few drops from the water cruet into the chalice. The only other time I had seen such a cup used was when I lived in Argentina. Most of the Italian churches did not use pews. They used straight-backed chairs.

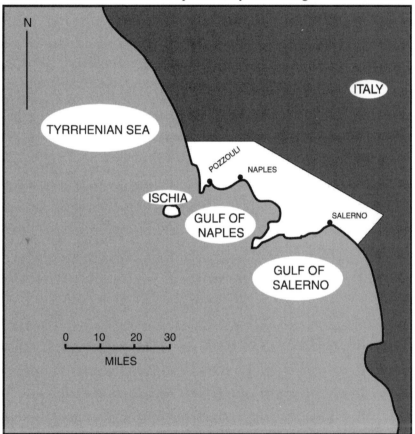

Fig 60. The Gulf of Naples which we almost entered while it was in German hands. The initial invasion was at the Gulf of Salerno.

An Officer's Bravado

A very comical event occurred after we had landed at Salerno. We had made several trips back and forth between North Africa and the

Salerno beachhead. We had orders to enter the harbor at Naples and discharge our cargo there. The opening into the harbor is very narrow. The Germans had sunk many ships with the intent of making it difficult to maneuver in the harbor and to unload our cargo.

Our convoy was in single file and was just about to enter the harbor when we received a message that the harbor was still held by the Germans. The convoy made a sharp right turn and headed south along the Italian coastline. We had to follow a certain course because of the sea mines that were under the surface of the water. Our course was along a path that previously had been cleared of mines by the mine sweepers and only a short distance from the shore (approximately one-half a mile). We were the third or fourth ship in line. It was a clear day and about 14:00 hours (2 PM).

We could hear the sounds of a German 88 mm artillery battery. We could also see the puffs of smoke from the guns. Therefore, we were able to determine approximately the location of this battery. We could determine when they fired as we could see the smoke. We did not have sufficient fire power; our fire power consisted of a few machine guns, several 20 mm rapid fire guns, several 40 mm anti-aircraft weapons, and a 3-inch-50 cannon. Consequently, we were unable to return fire at this battery. This latter armament was later changed to twin 40 mm's.

There were British troops on our ship on this particular trip and they had a captain as their commander. This captain had been in the army for several years and therefore was considered a wily veteran. He was very tall, about 6 foot 6 inches. The captain used the public address system to inform his troops that they should not be frightened and they were to follow his example. We were approaching the area where the Germans would be able to fire at us. We saw the smoke and heard the sound of the cannons. This British captain was so frightened that he tried to dig a fox hole into the steel deck. His troops just laughed themselves silly. The three shells just fell harmlessly away from the ship.

We continued until we were out of range before the Germans could reload and fire again. We traveled in a southerly direction to a safer location to discharge our cargo. We do not know if any of the ships behind us were hit. We never heard one way or another about their fate.

General Quarters

The klaxons would blast and an announcement over the loud speaker would order the sailors to go to our battle stations. The klaxon

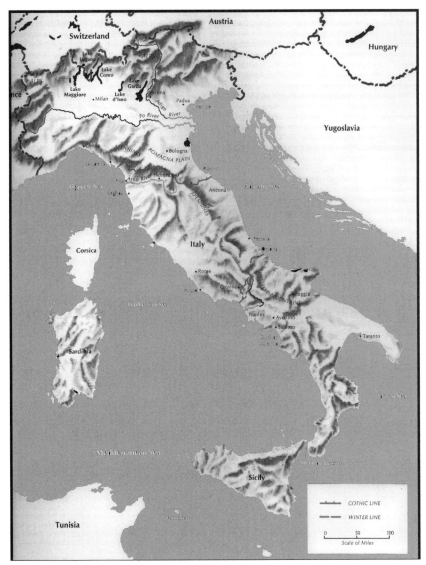

Fig 61. An overall view of Italy illustrating it's relation to various areas in the Mediterranean Sea.

is a combination of a shrill siren and a horn. The sound was so designed that you could not possibly mistake this sound for any other noise. I was a sound sleeper and would not hear the klaxon sound "General Quarters" The cook would awaken me, and I would wake with a start. Today I still wake with a start when someone wakens me from a sound sleep.

Normally, "General Quarters" indicated that you had a specific job to accomplish at a particular location. However, there were a few responsibilities during "General Quarters" that required that some functions be rotated. It was during one of these rotations that I encountered some heart-rending feelings.

A ship is composed of many air tight compartments. These compartments are all sealed off during "General Quarters." This particular time it was my function to go to the starboard side of the ship and close all the water tight doors, from amidships aft. Another sailor had the responsibility of closing the doors from amidships to the bow. Our orders were that we were not to wait for any one to clear out of a compartment but shut the doors immediately and lock them. There was one sailor that was working or sleeping in a compartment near the center of the ship at the time of "General Quarters." He just managed to get out before I closed the door. If he had waited a few seconds more he would have been locked in that compartment. The resultant consequences are difficult to predict. First, this sailor would not have reported to his battle station; second, if damage had affected that part of the ship he would have been trapped in that compartment. This very strict rule must be enforced without hesitation. It could be very crucial to the lives of the men on the ship. An air tight compartment with an open hatch completely defeats its purpose.

War Orphans

The harbor of Naples was finally taken from the Germans in October 1943 and we were able to enter the harbor on our next trip. We usually operated in and out of the Isle of Ischia (phonetically it is "ish why eeah"). The town of Pozzuoli was very near the isle. I also spent time at the local church performing the duties of an altar boy. There was an orphanage in this town and I spent much of my liberty at this orphanage. The children at this orphanage were the offspring of persons who had been killed in the war. The children at the orphanage were sure glad to see me. We played games (some of which I taught to them, and some they taught to me). If I could I would obtain some candy, chewing gum, or kitchen supplies. The nuns at the orphanage were most appreciative to receive these items. The item that the children really looked forward to was a chocolate bar. The times I spent with these children were most enjoyable to me.

"Jingle" Time

Our next invasion was at Anzio; code name for this operation was **"Jingle."** The date was January 22, 1944. This is a point where my memory failed me. It was during my recent research that the code name

Fig 62. LST 351 at Ischia unloading a group of German prisoners captured at Anzio.

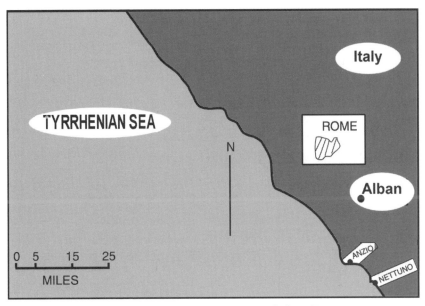

Fig 63. The landing area at Anzio and the distances to Alban Hills and Rome.

for this operation was "Shingle" and not "Jingle."

We were part of a decoy group. We continued north along the coast of Italy. That part of the convoy that included our ship was in sight of the mainland until we passed Anzio. This maneuver was to make the Germans think that the landing was to take place at Rome.

Fig 64. An overall view of Southern Italy Showing the landings at Licata, Salerno, and Anzio.

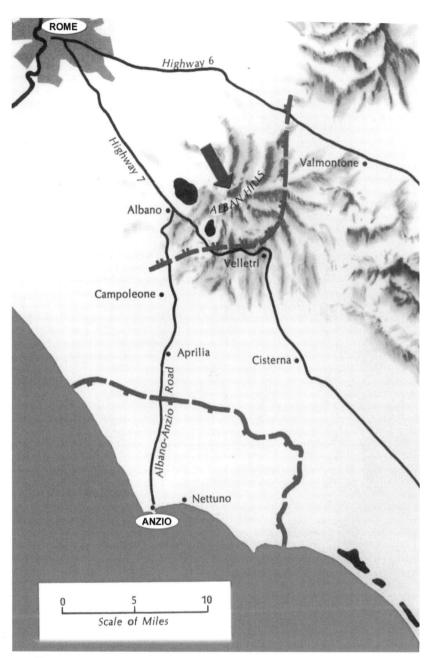

Fig 65. The distance of Anzio from Rome, and the location of the Alban Hills where the Germans fired their railroad cannon (275 mm). The lower dotted line was the limit of the beach head before breakout.

Rome is about twenty-five to thirty miles north of Anzio.

Anzio's sister town is called Nettuno. These twin towns were noted for their beaches and extravagant buildings and homes. These were the resort towns of Italy. (This area is similar to the Miami Beach section of Florida.)

We carried British Commandos on our ship, as part of our decoy operation we passed Anzio at dusk and when it became dark we turned around and headed back to Anzio. Our particular group landed at the northern most part of the landing beach.

A man took a small rubber boat almost up to the end of the jetty. He signaled the convoy using a covered, protected light. He informed us that the Germans were partying.

The invasion seemed to be a total success. The Allied leaders were hoping that the landing at Anzio would draw some of the German troops away from the fierce battle-taking place over Mount Cassino. Cassino was approximately seventy-five miles east. The natural terrain of mountains and rivers was making it extremely difficult for the Allies to advance, towards Rome. The losses at the Abbey of Cassino were very high.

The American Rangers and British Commandos were able to reach the outskirts of Rome. However, General Lucas did not wish to repeat those events that occurred at Salerno, where many of the American troops were cut off from the beach by the hidden Germans. The Rangers and Commandos met very little opposition but there was no follow-up by the regular troops. General Lucas elected to establish a beach-head and stay there. This delay gave the Germans adequate time to call their reserves and to mount a counter-attack. It also permitted the Germans to use a large railroad gun of 275 mm or about 11 inches in diameter.

A railroad gun is a very large cannon mounted on a railroad car that affords some degree of flexibility. The Germans could move the cannon from place to place. The one at Anzio was moved in and out of a cave. The Allied aviators had difficulty in spotting its location. It was located about 20 miles from the beachhead. The intent and purpose of this cannon was to bombard ships that were unloading their cargo. An artillery spotter would be situated where he could see the beachhead with his binoculars. He could radio instructions to the gunnery captain where to aim and fire to cause the most damage.

The Railroad Cannon

The Germans had two large cannons mounted on railroad cars. These cannons were probably being fired from the Alban Hills. These hills were approximately 15-20 miles away from the beachhead. The soldiers nicknamed them "Anzio Express" and "Anzio Annie." The 275 mm shells could inflict serious damage to the LSTs that were unloading their cargo. We were informed that a shell from a railroad cannon hit the deck of one of our LSTs and went right through to the bottom. It never exploded. This LST was very fortunate that the shell did not explode. This story demands many questions. Did the shell go through the bottom? Was that compartment flooded? What happened to the shell? Were temporary repairs performed? This happened at the beachhead at Anzio.

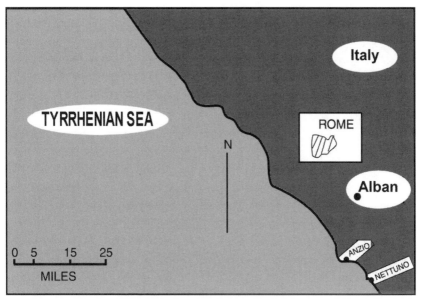

Fig 66. Sketch showing distances from Anzio to the Alban Hills and Anzio to Rome.

A Close Call

The Germans fired a shell from one of these eleven inch cannons . It exploded directly aft of our ship. The shell fragments made many holes in the stern bulkhead. There were several men nearby including myself. We were on the deck at the stern of the ship. Fortunately, none of the men were hurt. I was able to gather several more shrapnel fragments from this explosion. We began to pull in our stern anchor with the winch and at the same time reversed the engines. This is the normal procedure to back off a beach. We backed out of that precarious position before the Germans could load and fire again. The other LST that was next to us followed our example and backed out of the entrance. We moved out to the harbor away from the beach. The loading was completed utilizing the smaller landing craft acting as a shuttle service between the shore and our ship. We waited for a convoy to form and proceeded to Naples.

Fig 67. A water spout that was the result of the railroad cannon being fired from the Alban Hills. The close call LST 351 had experienced at Anzio was a copy of this shot.

The opening of the entrance into the Anzio harbor was very narrow, probably wide enough for two or three LSTs. We were one of two ships unloading at this narrow opening. The German artillery spotter for the railroad guns realized that if they could sink the two LSTs in this entrance it would block the entrance and it would be very difficult to unload directly onto the wharf any future LSTs . The unloading off shore is extremely slow. The railroad guns began firing at us, one shell landed about 100 feet astern of us. This explosion made many holes in our bulkhead but fortunately no one was injured. I still have shell fragments from this explosion. We accelerated the unloading of our moving cargo and completed the loading of some casualties. They were on their way to Naples for additional treatment. We backed out of this precarious position and headed out in the harbor. The LST next to us quickly followed us out.

Fig 68. Two LSTs loading return cargo at Anzio. There was only room for two LSTs.

A Challenge and the Reply

A world-wide recognition procedure was established for the Allies. Every six hours based upon Greenwich Mean Time, GMT, a set of recognition signals was determined and changed. A designated person in a central location changed the recognition codes. These codes were relayed to every military unit around the world. The challenge and the reply were sent by coded radio messages. These signals were established for several different situations: ship-to-ship, ship-to-plane, shore-to-ship, and shore-to-plane. The challenger sent by Morse code a set of two letters and was to receive two other letters. If the response was the correct letters then that indicated a friend. If the response was incorrect, that indicated foe and demanded the necessary action.

I was a signalman and it was my responsibility to remember these recognition signals. It was also my responsibility to know the exact time that these recognition signals changed. Another set of recognition signals was a set of three colored lights to be displayed vertically on each ship. These were for ship to ship, or ship to shore identification.

A German airplane was flying around the Anzio beachhead landing area and was challenged by one of the naval ships assisting with the landing. The German responded with the incorrect answer but nothing else happened. This German plane should have been fired upon, but was not.

A British Sunderland seaplane was flying in the area of the Anzio invasion. This seaplane was challenged in the normal manner by one of the naval ships. The correct response was returned but the ship fired on the plane. The plane was not shot down, but this mistake could have been disastrous. Many mistakes are made during battle.

A True Hero

Gene Bowen, the yeoman, mentioned above was on board the LCI during an invasion of the enemy shore. This LCI probably hit a sand bar and could not reach the dry land. Therefore, the water was over the soldiers' heads as they tried to go ashore. Several of these soldiers had difficulty with their heavy and bulky gear in the deep water. The yeoman helped many of these struggling soldiers. He assisted them until they could touch bottom. He swam with these soldiers that were struggling. His actions were similar to that of a lifeguard rescuing a drowning person. He probably saved several soldiers from drowning. It was for this feat that he was awarded the Navy Cross. This is the second highest award that an American sailor can earn.

Fig 69. A photo of an LCI not able to reach dry land. The soldiers had to wade towards shore. If the LCI hit a sand bar the soldiers could be in water over their head and with their gear could drown. This was the situation for Gene Bowen when he saved the lives of several soldiers.

A New Captain

Our merchant marine captain, who was our captain since the day of commissioning, was replaced by a "ninety-day wonder." This is the title that the sailors gave to someone who went to a Navy training program and was commissioned after ninety days of school. This captain brought with him a yeoman (a Navy secretary, typist, writer, etc.). His name was Gene Bowen. This yeoman had received the Navy Cross for his heroic action while he and the captain were aboard an LCI previous to their assignment with our ship.

Careful with Your Reply

This yeoman told us a story of an event that had occurred on the LCI. The captain came on the bridge at night time in the middle of a watch. There was a destroyer that was challenging the LCI. A return of the proper identification letters was in order. The captain asked the signalman on duty what letters he would send in response to the challenge. The signalman informed the captain of the two letters. The captain disagreed with the sailor and ordered him to send two other

Fig 70. The bow of an LCI and the unloading from man to man.

Fig 71. LCIs at sea. Each carries 200 infantry troops.

letters. The sailor obeyed the order. The destroyer then fired a shot across the bow of the LCI. The sailor promptly sent the correct letters. The destroyer then sent a message back to the LCI stressing the importance of a correct response. The recognition signals had changed during this sailor's watch and he had kept abreast of the changes; this is the responsibility of the signalman on watch. The captain did not realize that a change had taken place. The letters the captain ordered were from the previous time frame and almost meant disaster for his ship.

Fig 72. The prime purpose of an LST (Landing Ship Tanks) is to bring tanks to the enemy shore.

Fig 73. Soldiers unloading ammunition from two LCIs. Note: the ships could not reach dry land. This was often typical of the LCIs and other landing craft.

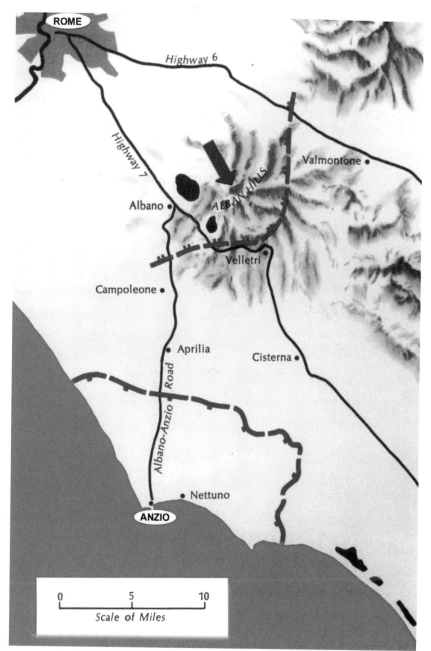

Fig 74. Battle map of the Anzio beachhead. The dotted line illustrates the Allied penetration.

Bombing and Shelling of the Hospital

The Hospital group set up their tents within the Anzio beachhead area. The center of the hospital was properly displayed with a huge red cross on a white background. This is according to the Geneva Convention to prevent the bombing of field hospitals. The Germans completely ignored this regulation and consistently bombed and shelled the hospital. It reminded me of the bombing of the British field hospital in Bougie. The Anzio landing area was so crowded and packed that it would become difficult to fire at the landing operation and not hit the hospital.

There was a rumor that an Allied hospital ship was transporting arms, an action also in violation of the Geneva Convention. It was also said that this gave the Germans the opportunity to retaliate.

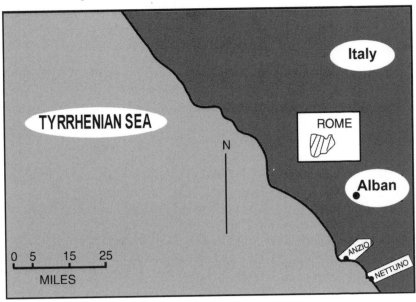

Fig 75. Sketch showing distances from Anzio to the Alban Hills and Anzio to Rome.

The National Geographic Magazine

We were unloading German prisoners onto the quay (I think) at Ischia. A photographer from the news media took a photograph of the front of our ship. The photograph illustrates the open bow doors with the ramp down. This occurred on another trip from Anzio. This picture that appeared in the National Geographic Magazine, in July 1944. The

Brightmoor Tabernacle Journal and some of the other printed media printed this picture of our ship. One of the news media sent me a copy of this photograph.

Fig 76. The proud ship, LST 351, (my ship) unloading German prisoners taken at Anzio. This photograph appeared in the July, 1944 issue of the National Geographic Magazine.

A Universal Language

I learned to play chess before I enlisted in the Navy. Some of the sailors aboard the ship could play. There were many times that I had the opportunity to practice my chess moves. We discovered that many of the Germans knew how to play also. I was engaged in this mind game with a German prisoner taken at Anzio. He did not understand English and I did not understand German but we found a mutual interest in the game of chess. We played several games. Then he defeated me with the "four move checkmate." I did not even know that such a series of moves existed. The Germans and the Poles defeated me more times at chess than I would win. It seemed that I had better success with the Italians and the English.

Army Shoes

It seemed that the Navy had difficulty in finding shoes that would fit me. I have a very short and wide foot. I obtained a pair of short Army boots that were very comfortable. However, these Army shoes were brown and the Navy requires black shoes. I polished and polished these shoes with black shoe polish. Most of the time I could pass inspection with these Army shoes.

Shell Shocked

It was during my single visit to Naples that I visited the USO. I met one of the American Rangers who participated in the invasion of Anzio. He was very disturbed and mentally shaken. He told me that five hundred of Darby's Rangers had participated in the invasion. He also stated that the Rangers were able to reach the outskirts of Rome and that a few of the men actually reached Rome. These Rangers were cut off from the rest of the troops as there was not any follow-up by the regular infantry. The balance of Darby's Rangers were either captured or killed. This was the result of the orders of the commanding general at Anzio. His name was General John P. Lucas. This soldier told me that there were only thirty-seven rangers who were able to return of the original 500. General Lucas was later replaced by General Truscott.

A Good Memory

It was about ten o'clock in the evening and I was the signalman on duty. The signalman reads the message while someone else records it. Since we were in port there was only one person (myself) on the bridge. We were planning to sail for Anzio the next morning. However, we took aboard a Navy commander and this made us the command ship of the next convoy. I did not know this information at the time. One of the ships wanted to send us a message and I tried to have them wait until I could get someone to write the message for me. This navy commander was standing behind me, and he told me to go ahead and receive the message. I took the message that contained fifty-seven words. I then had to write the whole message from memory. The commander asked to see the message before I took it to the captain.

He complimented me on my excellent memory and the manner in which I received the signal. He had read the Morse code right along with me.

We sailed that evening instead of waiting until morning. Our original orders were to load the ship and sail in the morning. However, the vehicles were ready before the appointed hour, and we were able to depart several hours earlier than originally planned.

A Rare Sight

We were returning from one of our trips to Anzio in the later part of March 1944. We were passing through the Naples harbor when we observed a tremendous sight. Mount Vesuvius was erupting.

We could see the lava flowing down the mountain side. The eruption and the flaming lava flow were fantastic to behold. It was a rare display of spouting lava and the devastation that happened as the lava flowed downhill.

Fig 77. The eruption of Mt. Vesuvius

Blinking Lights

Our second class signalman went into Naples on liberty and saw a stage play. One of the stage lights had a loose wire or connection and the light kept flickering. Our signalman began to read a Morse code message from this blinking light. One of the other sailors who was with him told us the story. He was accustomed to seeing blinking lights in the form of Morse code. He automatically began to make a message out of the loose wire connection. We sure kidded him over this incident for a long time. This event brought forth many laughs from the rest of the crew.

Tightrope Walker

There were usually three things that interested most sailors who were on liberty. They were women, whiskey, and gambling. I was one of the few sailors that did not follow this pattern. I went horseback riding several times while I was in North Africa. I enjoyed going into town and just walking around looking at the people and the buildings. I would visit churches or walk through some of the parks. I usually would look for a Chinese restaurant to eat in. I felt that I could get more food for my money.

There was a certain group on board our ship who swore they would get me drunk. I just avoided going on liberty with them. One evening we were returning from liberty and there was one sailor who was quite intoxicated. The ship was tied broadside along a pier. We will never know what prompted this sailor to do what he did next. There was a hawser (a hawser is a thick woven rope used for mooring the ship) from the stern of the ship tied to a bollard on the pier. A bollard is an upright metal post on a dock around which to fasten a rope. This sailor thought he could board the ship by walking along this hawser. Naturally, he fell into the water after his second step. The rest of us pulled him out of the water, then laughed ourselves silly.

Contract Bridge

Oswald Jacoby was a very famous bridge player. His grandson was stationed on board our ship and was somewhat of a braggart. He said his grandfather taught him the fine points of contract bridge. Bill Lane from Texas, and I played as bridge partners. Jacoby's grandson set forth a wager. He would teach some intelligent person on board how to play contract bridge and together they would take us to the cleaners. He spent several weeks teaching another sailor how to play contract bridge and then said that he and his partner were ready to play against us. We agreed upon his suggestion to keep a running score.

Bill and I created some highly unusual systems of bidding. Our unusual signaling to each other through our highly irregular bidding system gave us an advantage. Bill and I would often change our bidding techniques to confuse our opponents. We played bridge for several months. We reached a running total whereby Bill and I were 200,000 points ahead of our opponents. Jacoby gave up playing bridge against us at this point.

Troops Not Familiar with American Ways

It was during one of our longer trips that we took on board a number of unusual Allies. They were the Indian Sikhs. These soldiers had the reputation of being some of the best soldiers in the world. They each wore a turban. Their claim was that they were fearless and extremely daring. They could move quickly without any sound. We did not mix with them as they did not wish to socialize.

Consequently, this lack of communication led to an unsavory occurrence for our crew. These Sikhs did not know how to use a toilet. It seems that the commodes on our ship were the first they had ever seen. They were accustomed to squatting over a hole and relieving themselves. They attempted to duplicate this on the commodes. They squatted by standing on the sides of the toilets and then relieved themselves. The sea was rather rough this trip Therefore, you can imagine how many times they hit their target. We had to clean this mess after they had disembarked. The smell and mess were so bad that we had to enter the head area (the head is a sailors term for the bathroom) with gas masks and fire hoses. Some of the sailors cleaning up this mess actually became sick.

Section Eight

There was a sailor on board our ship who found a way to avoid future combat action. He would stand watch and juggle an imaginary ball. He would perform this function at some of the oddest moments but always when an officer was present. The captain finally transferred him to a naval base. This was done under what the Navy refers to as "Section Eight."-the regulation that stipulates the referral of a sailor to a hospital for a mental evaluation. The other sailors knew that this sailor was doing a good job of acting and thought that it was unfair to place this man under Section Eight.

Leave North Africa

We received sailing orders to return to Lake Bizerte, Algeria. Here we received orders to sail for England. We sailed with a convoy that included a number of other LSTs.

Our ultimate destination was Swansea, Wales. We arrived at Swansea after traveling several days. Another unusual event occurred as we were entering the harbor at Swansea. The entrance to the harbor was rather narrow. We had to pass very close to the moored ships. There was a projection on one of our LCVPs. This part was sticking out and it caught onto a hawser. No one noticed that this hawser was becoming tighter and tighter. This rope began to sing as the strain became very severe. There would be considerable damage to our ship if this was to continue and possible damage to the ship whose line became entangled with our small boat. I jumped down onto that small boat (the LCVP). I took out my knife and positioned myself so that I would be free of the line when it parted. The severe strain would result in a whip lash of this hawser as it was cut. I barely touched the line with my knife. It parted and whipped over my head. The strain on the line resulted in the sudden separation before I was fully prepared. I jumped to an awkward position to avoid the slashing line, and injured my leg. The pharmacist mate later said it was just a slight strain but it affected me for a long time thereafter.

Plymouth, England and Friends

The ship was loaded at Swansea with food, fuel, and miscellaneous supplies. We headed for Plymouth, England. The ship along with many other LSTs stayed at this port for several weeks. It was my first

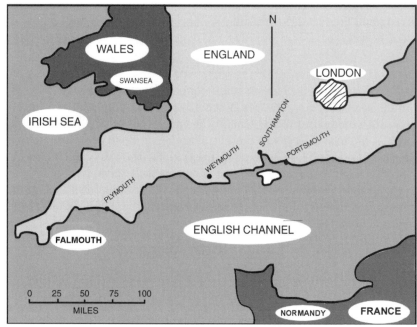

Fig 78. A sketch of southern England showing the location of several of the English ports. We sailed in an Easterly direction from Falmouth to the landing at Utah beach (Normandy).

liberty in England that I went into town and looked for a Catholic Church. There was a slight effort in understanding the speech of the English, but someone directed me to the nearest Catholic Church. It was only a few minutes' walk from the dock area. I rang the bell at the rectory and asked to speak with a young priest. The housekeeper, a Miss Cooper, thought that this was an unusual request. I explained to her that I was a Catholic American sailor and was not one for partying. I was only twenty-one years old. I thought that I could communicate with a younger priest better than with an older one. She told me that they were just beginning Benediction service and if I would stay, then she could talk to me after the service. I was told to go into the sacristy after the service. This housekeeper took me home. This was another ten minute walk. I met her sisters and some of her friends. Her youngest sister was fifty-six years old. I visited with this group of women many times. I never did have the opportunity to speak with the priest.

I would spend a few of my liberty evenings at the USO (United Service Organization) but mostly with the Coopers. I taught the Virginia Reel to the British during one of my visits to the USO. They really enjoyed this change of pace to their dancing.

Tea to an Irish Mother

It was during one of these visits that Miss Cooper introduced me to a friend from Ireland. This lady said that her mother in Ireland was having difficulty obtaining any tea. A cup of tea is as important to the Irish as it is to the English. The rationing was affecting the people in the British Isles more severely than the people in the United States. I managed to obtain her mother's address in Ireland and wrote to my mother in America to see if she could help me with a favor. I explained the difficulty with rationing of the tea.

My mother bought 8 ounces of tea and mailed it to Ireland. Imagine how the Irish lady felt when she heard that her mother had received 8 ounces of tea. My Irish friend heard from her mother after she had received that unusual gift. It was very difficult to obtain one ounce of tea in Ireland. This Irish friend was forever grateful. I corresponded with the Cooper family of sisters for many years after I received my military discharge. However, I lost contact with this family when I moved to Argentina in 1966.

Honey and Dandelion Wine

The Cooper sisters suggested that I spend a weekend at the Buckfast Abbey which was a short bus ride from Plymouth. They made arrangements for me to visit the Abbey. The monks there are famous for their bee-keeping, their honey, and their dandelion wine. I did visit this wonderful church when I had a weekend liberty. I arrived on a Friday afternoon and returned on Monday morning.

I had the opportunity to observe the monks with their bees and saw how dandelion wine was produced. The monks kept me well occupied during my stay. The monk that was in charge of the bee-keeping took a special attachment to me. Fifty years later I had a very pleasant surprise. I was watching an educational TV program about bee-keeping, and I saw this monk who had taken a special interest in me. This monk is world famous for his knowledge of bees and honey.

Fig 79. The west view of the Buckfast Abbey famous for it's honey and dandelion wine.

Next Invasion

We were berthed in Plymouth for several weeks before we received orders to load the ship. Naturally, we also received our set of inoculations. These shots were not according to the regular schedule. We knew that this meant another invasion would be coming. We loaded our main deck with various types of moving vehicles. Our tank deck was loaded with the usual tanks. It takes one to two days to completely load an LST. We left Plymouth and sailed west to enter the harbor of Falmouth. Here we awaited further orders. There was a severe storm that delayed our sailing by one day. The delay created some tension among all the military personnel. No one was permitted to go ashore. Finally, General Eisenhower said that the invasion would take place on June 6. We left Falmouth and joined up with a convoy to cross the English Channel.

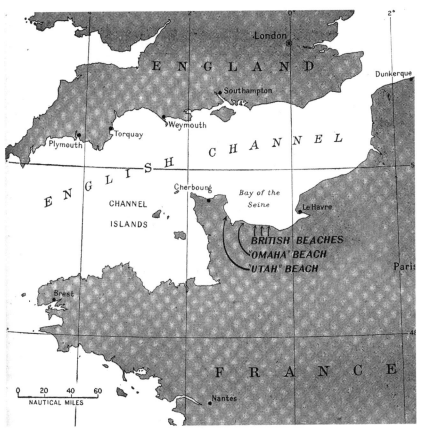

Fig 80. The five Allied beaches at Normandy; Utah, Omaha, Gold, Juno, Sword. We landed at the Western most beach at Utah.

"D-Day"

It was on June 5, 1944 that we sailed for the coast of France from the port of Falmouth. Falmouth is the most western port from which ships sailed for the Normandy invasion. The next morning the invasion of France commenced. This was the largest invasion of a foreign territory in the history of the world. It became known throughout the world as **"D-DAY."**

Military Leak or a Coincidence

A secondary operation of the invasion was given the code name Neptune. This was primarily related to the paratroops and glider troops landing behind the lines . Their operation was to capture some villages and cut off the Germans from bringing up reserves.

During the five weeks prior to "D-Day", five crossword puzzles in London's Daily Telegraph horrified the SHAEF generals. Each contained s secret word directly related to the impending invasion of Normandy: "Utah", "Omaha", "Mulberry", "Neptune", and "Overlord."

Fig 81. 17 across—
One of the U.S.

The appearance of "Overlord" convinced the invasion planners that security had been breached. Scotland Yard detectives questioned the puzzle compiler, Leonard Dawe. They discovered that he was an unassuming physics teacher who composed crosswords as a hobby. Dawe was convincingly bewildered by the interrogation, and the investigation finally drew the conclusion that it was an amazing coincidence. There was no leak.

"Overlord and Neptune"

Our sailing from Falmouth put us in position to form up with the western-most convoy. The five beaches at Normandy where the invasion would ultimately take place were given five code names: UTAH, OMAHA, GOLD, JUNO, and SWORD.

The assault phase of Operation Overlord began shortly after midnight on June 6, when three Allied airborne divisions; the British

6th; U.S. 82nd and U.S. 101st; landed in Normandy. Their objective was to secure vital inland targets in preparation for the amphibious assault. Between 6:30 and 7:35 a.m., leading elements of five Ameri-

Fig 82. 11 across — but some bigwig like this has stolen some of it at times

can, British and Canadian divisions hit invasion beaches. Though the Allies established beachheads and seized many of their targets in each sector, they met with stiff resistance from the German forces-deployed as shown-and were prevented from taking their most important "D-Day" objective, the city of Caen. Every operation of the war on both sides was given a code name. The code name for the overall invasion of France was called Overlord.

Fig 83. 15 across— Britania and he hold to the same thing

Fig 84.
3 down —
Red Indian
on the
Missouri

The Americans were to land at Utah and Omaha. The British, Canadians, and Polish forces were to land at the eastern most beaches; code named Gold, Juno, and Sword.

Fig 85. 11 across— This bush is a center of nursery revolutions

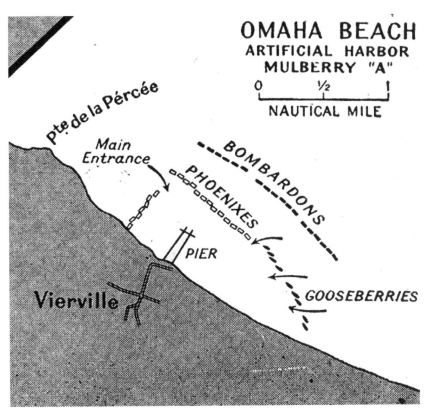

Fig 86. The artificial harbors were code named "Mulberry". This is one of the words used in the crossword puzzle.

Unique System of Identification

The airborne troops would land behind the lines during the darkness. A solution to identify friend or foe was devised: each of the airborne troops carried a clicking device to identify friends. One click answered by two clicks meant that the other man was a friend.

The airdrop was so far off track that it confused the Germans. They were not sure where the invasion was going to take place. Hitler still believed that the landing would take place at Pas de Calais. This would be the shortest distance across the channel. Hitler also believed that General Patton would lead the invasion. The Allies had a plan to make Hitler believe that the crossing would be towards Pas de Calais. General Patton was seen in the eastern part of England. There were also hundreds and hundreds of fake tanks and trucks stored in the eastern part of England. These fake trucks and tanks were made out of

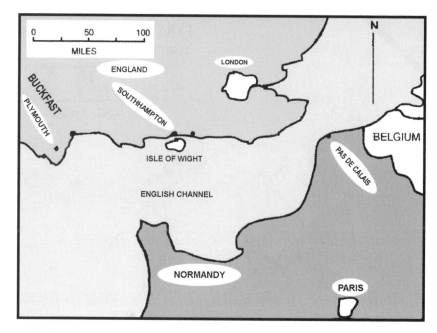

Fig 87. The shortest distance across the English Channel occurs at Pas de Calais. The Germans believed that the invasion would take place here.

cardboard, rubber, and wood. It was difficult to distinguish the difference during an aerial reconnaissance.

Planes Beyond Comprehension

There was one four-hour period that I was on watch as we crossed the English Channel and B-24s were flying over our ship. These bombers were visible when I came on watch at noon and were still visible when I went off watch at 16:00 (four PM). It is very difficult to comprehend the enormous number of planes that flew overhead during this four-hour span. All aircraft were painted with three white stripes on the wings or on the fuselage. This permitted the naval forces and the ground troops to recognize friendly aircraft immediately. Thus, no need for a challenge and a reply.

We sailed across the English channel without any specific incident. The circumstance of my regular watch and the ordering of General Quarters for our ship was rather unfortunate for me. I was coming off watch and was ready to grab some shuteye when the order came over the public address system for General Quarters.

The sailors on board our ship realized that another invasion was

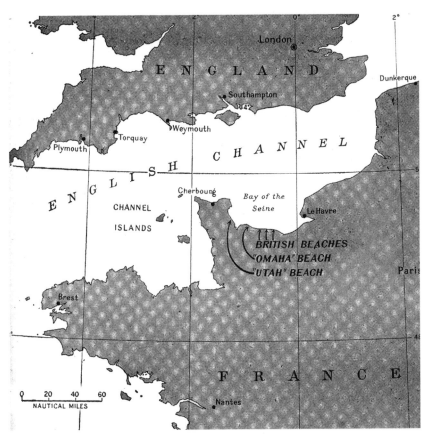

Fig 88. The five Allied beaches at Normandy; Utah, Omaha, Gold, Juno, Sword. We landed at the Western most beach at Utah.

going to take place. We tried to get some sleep but the stress and tension made it almost impossible. There were very few men on our ship who had been able to get any sleep from the time we had entered Falmouth harbor. We had expected to sail on the 4th for the landing of the 5th. There was a very bad storm and it appeared that we would be delayed several days. The meteorologist informed General Eisenhower that there would be a break in the weather on the 6th. The general had a very difficult decision to make. Do we land on the 6th or extend the delay? It is very difficult to keep an operation of this magnitude secret for any length of time.

Most of the above information was obtained from the writings of authors after the actual invasion. Much of this information was very secret and confidential for many years. Some statements were received from the casualties; but you could not rely on its authenticity.

French Waters

We dropped anchor in the darkness somewhere off the French Normandy coast. This is about 140 miles southwest from Pas de Calais. There was a time after we anchored that we had to wait for the proper time, "H-Hour", to lower our small boats. It takes some time to load 36 infantry troops into each of six LCVPs. It takes an even longer time to load twenty or more LCVPs from the Attack Transports. "H-Hour" requires that the actual landing of the first wave of troops be coordinated to the degree that all troops are approaching the beach at the identical time.

The Softening Up Process

There was a British battleship either the Rodney or the Nelson lying outboard of the position where we were anchored. This battleship was continually firing its big cannons (nine-16-inch guns). These big shells were flying directly over our ship. The sound of the guns firing and the explosion of these shells was deafening. We could even hear the whistle of the shells as they passed over us. We witnessed the introduction of a new Allied weapon. This was an LCT outfitted with rocket racks. This boat could fire one thousand 5-inch rockets in four minutes. The sound from these rockets was deafening. The light trails were a sight to behold. A tremendous fireworks display was observed (a tracer round of ammunition is fired at regular intervals). A destroyer moved in quite close to the beach and bombarded some of the installations. We were afraid that this destroyer would run aground.

Fig 89. Underwater obstacles similar to those seen at Normandy.

Low Tide Confuses the Germans

The Normandy landing took place at low tide. The Germans never suspected that a landing would take place at low tide. The invasions of Sicily, Salerno and Anzio were all done at high tide.

Fig 90. Some log underwater obstacles on the beaches at Normandy. General Rommel was placed in charge of building the beach fortifications and he utilized what ever materials were available to attain his objective.

Fig 91. More underwater obstacles similar to those encountered at Mont-St-Michele.

The distance to cover to the beach would thus be greater. The small boats have an advantage at low tide or shortly thereafter. The obstacles or the impediments buried below the surface of the water could be seen at something less than high tide. Then these underwater obstacles could be avoided. Many of these underwater obstacles were designed to tear a hole into the bottom of any boat passing over them. They were usually made of a steel beam with a pointed end facing out to sea. They were often imbedded in a concrete base.

The UDT (Underwater Demolition Teams) teams could remove some of these underwater obstacles and the attached mines to permit the larger LSTs to land on the beach without problems.

If the initial landing of the infantry took place at low tide then these troops would have longer to wait for some of their mechanized support, such as the heavy trucks and the tanks. These could only be unloaded when the LST had beached, near high tide. A few tanks could be unloaded from LCTs These boats could carry one tank at a time.

We lowered our six LCVPs at the appointed time. These LCVPs circled and joined with several other small boats. The group of

Fig 92. More underwater obstacles to deter, damage or slow down the incoming landing craft.

soldiers that would be part of the first wave to land on enemy soil came from the LSTs and the Attack Transports (APA). These APAs also carried LCVPs. A number of these LCVPs would circle until their entire group were assembled. This circle of LCVPs and several similar circles would become the initial thrust force of infantry troops to land on the unfriendly shore of France.

Half of a Safe Path

Our ship was anchored and we were awaiting the proper time to make a run at the beach to unload our mobile cargo. There were many ships that were traveling in an apparent safe lane. The mine sweepers would clear a certain section of under water mines. This path then would permit the ships to approach the beach safely. However, something unusual happened; a fair number of ships moving in this apparent safe lane were blown up by underwater mines. Some of these ships were sunk in less than two minutes. This indicates the power of these mines. An LST is approximately 350 feet long. One LST that struck one of these powerful mines broke in two and sank to the bottom. The force of the blast and the currents caused the bow to separate from the stern by a great distance. We could see the mast and the forward flag pole as they settled on the bottom. These two items were sticking up out of the water as the depth of the sea at that point was not enough to completely cover the ship. The mast and flag pole were over one thousand feet apart.

We had heard later that the mine sweepers swept the wrong path. The area that was to be safe for movement of the ships was only approximately one half of the designated section. This is the reason that a large number of ships were sunk by these mines. The Admiral in charge of this operation was named Moon.

High and Dry at Normandy

The tide depth in Normandy was about twenty-five feet. The LST has to land on the beach after high tide because at the time of withdrawal the water under the ship at high tide aids in the backing off the beach. This great tidal change is very significant as a ship the size of an LST would be sitting high and dry on the beach.

D-Day Activities

The amount of different activities that were taking place at the same time was innumerable. There were fighter planes flying back and forth trying to protect the men on the beaches. Ships were being sunk by mines or from shore batteries. There was considerable activity on the beach. The immensity of the entire landing operation was a matter of incomprehensible logistics. This activity appeared to be a hodgepodge but was generally proceeding according to a pre-arranged plan. There was considerable firing of guns, rockets, and cannons. The noise was deafening. Fortunately, the German Air Force did not have many planes in the air during the invasion. The Allied air superiority was very much in evidence; we were very thankful for this.

"Utah Beach"

We had a fairly good view of the beach from our ship as dawn arose. We could see several small buildings that appeared to be private homes. The one feature of the landscape which the soldiers often mentioned was the hedgerows. These were made of very thick bushes that probably had been growing for many years. These bushes were so thick that they could not be penetrated, normally. There were some openings but the German soldiers would be waiting in ambush at these openings. The area behind these hedgerows was also flooded at the time of the invasion. The combination of these hedgerows and the flooding made it extremely difficult to advance. American ingenuity solved this problem of the hedgerows. They equipped tanks with a special gadget that would cut through these hedgerows. We heard of this achievement from some of the returning soldiers.

Fig 93. An LST high and dry on a Normandy beach. The result of 27 foot tide levels. This situation generated a very helpless feeling to the sailors on board the LSTs.

Fig 94. This is what the enemy sees as the invasion landing craft approach the foreign shore.

Wrong Area Leads to an Advantage

There was another story we heard from the returning invaders. The initial landing at Utah actually took place at the wrong location. General Roosevelt was part of this group, therefore the highest ranking officer in this area. He was the son of former President, Theodore Roosevelt. General Roosevelt made the decision that the Utah beach landing would begin "here." Fortunately, as it was later determined that this was an important decision. The area that was incorrect was not heavily protected and an advance towards the hedgerows began with very few casualties.

Our particular beach (Utah) was relatively flat. We could see some German signs that read "minen." We knew that area had been mined. We wondered if the American troops with the metal detectors had cleared the area. We did not intend to go ashore to find out. However, we could see a cliff to our left. We later learned that this cliff was called Pont du Hoc. Pont du Hoc had to be scaled by the Rangers to silence several large cannons at the top of this cliff. This Ranger group lost half of their men during the scaling of the cliffs. Later we learned that there were no huge canons at Pont do Hoc. The supposed cannons were at another location. Pont du Hoc was located between the Utah and Omaha beachheads. I was able to visit Pont du Hoc in 1995.

Improved Utilization

The initial deployment of LSTs was somewhat haphazard. An LST would load up with whatever was closest to the ship. Therefore, a returning LST would be carrying a mixture of prisoners, casualties, etc. Someone finally figured a system to make the LSTs more efficient. An LST usually carried one pharmacist mate. However, during an invasion each LST would carry two or three doctors. There were also additional pharmacist mates. Then on a return trip one LST would be designated to carry prisoners. The additional medical personnel on this LST would be transferred to another LST that was designated to carry the casualties.

The entire system of shuttling supplies back and forth to the last beachhead was enhanced by this change. After discharging our cargo we would make the return trip with either prisoners or casualties.

One Thousand Prisoners

We backed off the beach and anchored out in deep water to await further orders. It was dark. We were also awaiting a convoy to form for the return to England. We received instructions from the command ship to receive one thousand German prisoners to be transported to England. The prisoners came aboard and we put them into our tank deck.

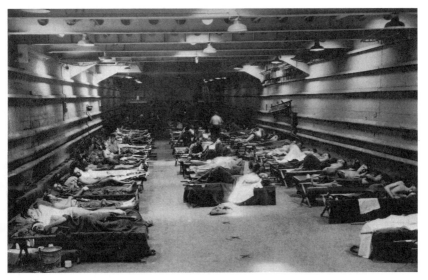

Fig 95. The tank deck on our ship similar to this one, contained 1000 German prisoners taken at Normandy to be delivered to England.

Two Hundred Casualties

We transferred all the extra medical personnel to another LST. I was the signalman on duty at this time. I received a message from the convoy command ship that stated, "Be prepared to take aboard 250 American casualties." I attempted to inform the convoy command ship that we already had 1000 prisoners on board. There would not be room for casualties. This is the area normally for the casualties but our tank deck was filled with prisoners. The return message stated it was too late, the casualties were already on their way. "You should do the best you can under the present circumstances."

We received one compliment of medical help from another LST. This was still less than we would have carried to handle 250 casualties. We started to load the casualties. They were placed on the floor, in the enlisted men's bunks and in every available space that could be found.

There were some men placed on the top deck and there were even a few in the signaling area. Most of these casualties were either paratroopers or glider troops. I was administering morphine to a number of the wounded. The morphine came in ampoules. We had to mark on a person's forehead the date, the time and the dosage of the last morphine administered. This system was employed to avoid over-dosage. The marking on the forehead was usually done with mercurochrome or metaphen. These solutions are antiseptics. The red color made it easy to read the information when painted on the bare skin.

A few of the casualties developed gangrene. This produces the vilest odor imaginable. I heard that our ship did not lose any of our casualties. I was extremely busy. I assisted the wounded. I would change dressings, administer morphine, give some of the soldiers blood plasma, or just talk and comfort them. A paratrooper who had both ankles crushed was placed in my bunk. He had two large wire supports fastened to his ankles. These wire supports were about eighteen inches in diameter and were directly below his feet. He was unable to walk. The wire frames were placed there by a doctor in an advanced medical facility, similar to MASH. I had several opportunities to speak with this soldier. I tried to make him feel more at ease. He was fairly well sedated. He was one of the soldiers to whom I had to administer a dose of morphine. He explained that his parachute was designed to hold two hundred and eighty pounds. He estimated that his weight, plus all of his equipment, (guns, ammunition, etc.) was in excess of three-hundred pounds. The Germans were firing at him during his descent. There were many holes in his parachute. He himself was not hit. However, the excess weight and the holes in his parachute caused him to descend considerably faster than was safe. Consequently, he broke both of his ankles at the moment of impact. We often wondered if this paratrooper would be eligible for the Purple Heart.

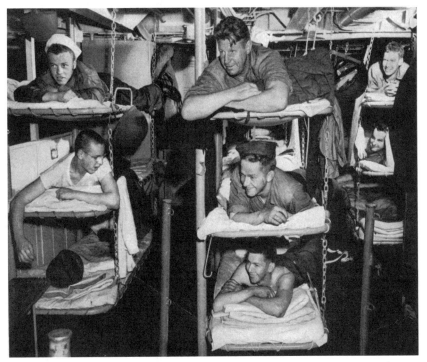

Fig 96. This was our sleeping quarters or bunks aboard our LST. I had the lower bunk, and the cook had the upper one. There was only sufficient height at this spot for two bunks. There were some areas that the bunks were four high.

Guard Duty and a Bold German

There was a period of almost five days that I had little or no sleep. A convoy was formed and we headed to England. My assignment was to guard the German prisoners. The prisoners were placed in our tank or lower deck. I would stand my regular watch for four hours, then guard the prisoners for another four hours; then assist the wounded for the next four hours. Then the cycle would be repeated. It was during my first guard duty that a somewhat frightening event occurred. There was a yellow line painted on the tank deck. It was explained to the German prisoners, in German, that they were not to cross this line. My position of guarding was on the other side of this yellow line. I had a rifle with a bayonet at my belt.

There was another sailor on duty with me. He was armed in a similar manner. The bow door and ramp were closed and locked at the opposite end. There were two sailors stationed at the stairs that led to the upper deck. Each had a Thompson .45 caliber sub-machine gun. The only exit then was the stairs behind us. These four sailors would be no match if the Germans decided to rush us. Therefore, it was emphasized to us to keep the Germans behind the designated line.

There was one obstinate prisoner who consistently tried to cross the line. He would step over then step back. Each time he became bolder and bolder and step farther and farther over the yellow line. I tried to push him back with the rifle held crosswise against his chest but to no avail. My partner and I thought that the situation was becoming desperate. What should we do? Then I remembered that most Germans were afraid of a bayonet. I took the bayonet from my belt and fastened it to the end of the rifle. I pointed the bayonet at this obstinate German but he still insisted in crossing the line. I touched him in the butt as he turned from me. He turned back and snarled at me and felt his rear. This German soldier never tried to cross the line after this incident.

Admirals Commendation

The Admiral decided to honor me with an award for the efforts above and beyond the call of duty for treating the wounded; administering Morphine and blood plasma, cleaning and dressing wounds, and consoling the injured.

The statement of the commendation is as follows: "The Flotilla Commander notes with pleasure the report of your excellent performance of duty during the night of 8 June 1944 (D-plus-2). You are commended for your untiring cooperation in rendering aid to the wounded on this occasion. This fine spirit is in keeping with the best practices of the service."

Four other sailors and I received the Admiral's Commendation for our efforts during this invasion.

Photos Do Not Tell The Whole Story

The soldiers that landed in the gliders had another story to tell. The allied planes and gliders were painted with three white stripes. This permitted rapid identification of the friendly planes. A photo reconnaissance plane had taken pictures of the purported landing area for the gliders. The photos indicated that the fields were clear. However, at the time of landing there were trees, poles, rocks, and many other obstacles to impede their landing. These obstacles were placed there during the night.

The gliders were made of plywood and were towed behind a plane. The glider or gliders were released and the pilot would attempt to steer it onto the designated field. The glider is just as the name implies. There is no motor and the pilot is very limited in his ability to maneuver.

Each of our casualties had his story to tell, and fifty years later I cannot remember all of them. There were stories of the paratroopers landing in the wrong area, of becoming separated from their unit. This mix-up of the landing areas of the paratroopers also confused the Germans. There were many disrupted incoming reports relative to the airborne landings. The scattered nature of these reports made it difficult to determine what was taking place and where. The clicking device that the paratroopers carried was very ingenuous. The soldiers stated it was a simple device to separate friend from foe. This device is demonstrated in the movie "The Longest Day."

<u>"Omaha Beach"</u>

The first time I saw the Omaha beach area I was amazed that the American soldiers were able to advance. There was a cliff approximately two hundred feet high. There did not seem to be any opening for

Fig 97. LSTs on the Omaha beach at Normandy on "D-Day".

the American soldiers to pass through without climbing the cliffs. The German Army had heavily secured all of the beaches of Normandy. We could see huge bunkers at the top. The bunkers had openings that faced seaward. The guns that protected a portion of the beach protruded through these openings. The buildings were constructed so that they were protected from shells and bombs. Portions of these bunkers were underground, connected to storage areas, mess halls, and living quarters by underground tunnels. The area was close to becoming an underground city and it appeared that the bunkers could fire across our entire landing area. These bunkers held some fairly large cannons. It is readily seen why there were so many casualties at the Omaha beachhead landing. The bunkers at Pont du Hoc could only hold smaller guns, mainly machine guns. I confirmed this fact 50 years later during my visit to France in September 1995.

There was another bad storm, probably "D-Day" plus ten or fifteen. The result was that many more ships were wrecked during this

Fig 98. A typical bunker as part of the German Atlantic wall in Normandy.

storm. There were shipwrecks all over the landing area at the Omaha beachhead.

A Signal Confirmation Averts Disaster

It was during another crossing of the English Channel that I was coming on watch at approximately 11:30. The signalman on duty was taking a Morse code message by light. He requested that I write down the message for him. This signalman told me that the message read as follows: "prepare to beach at 12:50." I read the message along with this signalman but the time that I read was 17:50. (Two in Morse code is two dots and three dashes[..---] and seven is two dashes and three dots[--...]). I requested the signalman to ask for a confirmation. He temporarily balked at this suggestion but finally relented. The return confirmed message did indicate that the correct time was 17:50. This slight error could have been very serious. We would have been stranded on the beach if we had gone in at the earlier time. Finally we ran our ship onto the beach and unloaded our mobile cargo.

The tides in this area are about twenty-five feet. Our ship only draws twelve feet. Consequently, at the time of low tide (the water has receded to its lowest depth), our ship is sitting on dry land. The sailors refer to this as sitting high and dry. This condition made all of us feel uneasy, as we were then "sitting ducks" for any German airplanes.

<u>"Mulberry"</u>

The attempted landing at Dieppe in August 1942 made it very plain that any harbor area would be highly protected. The time and the loss of life would be very high if there was to be an attempt to capture an existing harbor. Therefore, it was imperative that an artificial harbor or harbors be created. The British arrived at an unusual solution: they made a structure of concrete and steel. There were hundreds of these structures. They were usually towed across the English Channel by sea-going tugs. The formation of an artificial harbor was given the code name "Mulberry". The one that received the most notoriety was at Arromanches-les-bains, a seaside resort. It was here that many of the pre-fabricated structures were sunk to form an artificial harbor. This harbor-causeway was constructed far enough out to sea that the LST's could unload and load and not have to be concerned with the tides. There was a saving of considerable time with this operation.

However, another attempt to establish an artificial harbor, named Mulberry-A broke up during a severe storm. It appears that the artificial harbor constructed by the American engineers failed. The failure of this second artificial harbor was probably due to the weather conditions and the unfamiliarity of the American engineers with this type of structure.

Benedictine Abbey

Fig 99. More underwater obstacles similar to those encountered at Mont-St-Michele.

We landed supplies behind the lines at a place called Mont-St-Michele. There is a very famous abbey built at Mont-St-Michele, which becomes an island at high tide. I do not remember seeing this famous abbey at that time. However, I was fortunate to visit the abbey during my return visit to France in 1995. The underwater impediments were plentiful. The obstacles seemed to be more numerous here than at Normandy. I believe it was the responsibility of the UDT (Underwater Demolition Team) group to clear a path for the incoming ships. We unloaded our cargo and were awaiting orders to return to England.

An American soldier was brought on board and placed under heavy guard. He was being returned to England for a possible court of inquiry into an investigation of his actions. The story we obtained from the guards concerning the prisoner was somewhat bizarre. The Germans had captured or obtained a number of American uniforms. Therefore, Germans dressed in the American uniforms were mingling with the

Fig 100. More underwater obstacles similar to those encountered at Mont-St-Michele. Note: the armed guard walking between the I beam obstacles, during low tide.

American troops. This situation could cause considerable havoc. The guards informed us that this American soldier approached an individual and spoke to him. He either let the soldier go or shot him; apparently determined by the soldier's reply. This soldier had killed ten to fifteen apparent German soldiers in this manner.

Avranches

It appears that our landing behind the lines at Mont-St-Michele was the beginning of a supply line for General Patton. He was the general that led an armored division across France. One of the towns he liberated was named Avranches. There was a young boy, 10 years old, who lived in that town at the time of the liberation. This boy was named John Lehodey. Today he is the president of the Sofitel Hotel chain in the United States. He desired to show his appreciation to those Americans who partook in the liberation of France. Mr. Lehodey invited on June 6, 1994 all the Normandy veterans and any member of Patton's Third Army to a dinner at one of his hotels. I enjoyed his hospitality at his hotel in Chicago. There were 350 veterans there. This is one of his seven hotels in the United States in which he demonstrated his generosity. We estimate that he served over 2000 dinners that evening. He arrived at his hotel in Chicago after hosting a similar event at the hotel in Minneapolis. General Westmoreland was the principal speaker. General Westmoreland was one of the top military leaders in Vietnam. Mr. Lehodey also made arrangements for a USO type show at our dinner party.

Merci

Mr. Lehodey had a poster made which he gave to each of the men that attended the dinner. This poster contained the names and signatures of the present-day school children from Avranches. Each student had written his or her thanks to the American soldiers who had liberated their town fifty years earlier. This poster states; "Les sanglots longs des violons de automne bercent mon couer d'une langueur monotone". [These were the code words that rang through the country-side signaling that the famous Normandy invasion was soon to come].

It was during June of 1944 and for many months after, many children were saved through the sacrificial giving of American soldiers who gave their rations to the local families whose homes and food supplies had been taken to outfit the Axis forces.

Today, the youth of France still remember the selfless giving of the American military forces and they commemorate the gallant acts and legacy of goodwill that was left behind. The caption on the poster indicates the "MERCI" afforded by the thirty-two children in the Ecole Elementaire d' Avranches. These children send their appreciation and gratitude to those being honored. They will remember and tell their children. I prize this poster very highly. This appreciation was demonstrated to me at another occasion. I was having lunch in Caen, France during my visit in 1995. There was a Frenchman sitting across of me. We were speaking about the Normandy invasion; my traveling partner mentioned that I was part of the initial landing at Normandy. The gentleman across from me stood up, saluted and said thank you! I wonder why there was a certain glow in my heart.

Mock D-Day Invasion

The city of Chicago sponsored a mock invasion at the Montrose Beach in June of 1994 in honor of the 50th anniversary of "D-Day". Mayor Daly of Chicago was also present.

I met a gentleman from Chicago at this mock invasion demonstration. He also landed at Normandy with the paratroops. We have maintained contact which each other. His name is Colonel James

Young. He was a t/sgt during his days as a "Pathfinder." This is a paratrooper that jumps first and helps to guide the balance of the airborne troops to their designated landing area. This is a very dangerous function. He later received a battlefield commission. He remained in the Army and ultimately attained the rank of a full colonel.

Intercepted Message

We had made another crossing to Normandy and were anchored in the bay. We were waiting for orders to discharge our cargo. I was the signalman on duty and had just received a message from another LST. The captain of this other LST was a close friend of our captain. The message was as follows: "What is the uniform of the day?" The message was relayed to our captain. Our captain's reply was: "The uniform of the day is flat hats, skivvies, and fur lined jock straps". Shortly after I sent this reply I received a message from the command ship, the Ancon. Their signalman had intercepted our reply and cautioned us that we should be more careful concerning visual messages that we sent. You never know who will intercept your messages. All of these messages were sent by Morse code using lights.

A Crooked Picture

The soldiers we took back to England had many stories to tell. One in particular was relative to the Americans fetish to straighten out pictures on the wall. They told a story of a group of soldiers that had entered a building situated in an area previously occupied by the Germans. There was a picture on the wall that was askew. One of the American soldiers went to the wall to straighten the picture. The Germans knew that most Americans could not stand the appearance of a crooked picture. The picture in this building was booby-trapped. This means that if anyone would attempt to straighten the picture a bomb would explode. The building blew up at the time the soldier tried to straighten the picture. One of the soldiers was killed.

The Germans found many ways and items on which to set booby-traps. Military articles and watches were especially used. The medals, particularly the Iron Cross or any other medal, were fascinating to the American soldier and could be booby-traps.

Tilbury and Harrods

We continued to make channel crossings and return to England. There were a number of ports that we entered for reloading: Plymouth, Portsmouth, South Hampton, and London.

The Thames river stop for the LSTs was a town called Tilbury.

We stopped at Tilbury after one of our crossings. I was one of the fortunate ones who was given liberty to go in to London. Several other sailors and I reported back to the pier on time. The ship was gone when we arrived. The ship had received sailing orders while we were on liberty. The sailors had to be classified as AWOL in spite of the fact we came back on time. I guess you would call this the fortunes of war. We had to wait at this port until arrangements could be made to get us back to our ship. Fortunately, the ship had traveled further up the Thames to pick up some cargo then returned to our berth at Tilbury.

I shopped at Harrods during one of my liberty trips to London. I purchased an Irish linen tablecloth for my mother. I pondered as to how I would be able to send her this tablecloth. Someone suggested sending it in a cigar box. I obtained a cigar box. I had to fold and unfold the tablecloth repeatedly. I finally succeeded in fitting it into the cigar box.

My mother returned that tablecloth to me, thirty years later.

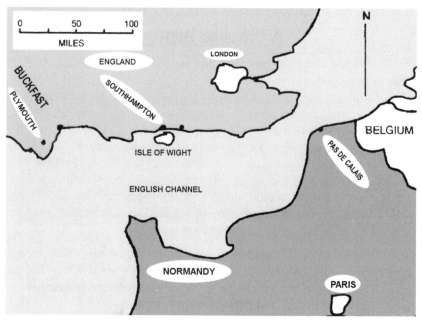

Fig 101. Sketch of southern England illustrating the distance from the White Cliffs of Dover to the French Port, Pas de Calais. It was here that Hitler thought that the invasion would take place. General Patton seen with a fake army in the southern part of England aided in this deception.

Secret Weapons (V-1)

The Germans had developed a new weapon, called the **V-1** rocket bomb. We saw it for the first time during one of our channel crossings. It was a rocket without a pilot, with wings and a very explosive warhead. There was a gyroscope on board to assist this bomb in level flight. The British termed it the buzz bomb. This name was assigned to this oddly shaped flying bomb because of the noise it made during flight. We sailors dubbed it the flying smokestack as there was a smoke trail coming out of the rocket portion of this new weapon. The rocket portion was fastened to the bomb portion by a system of struts. The fighter pilots tried to shoot these V-1 bombs so that they would explode or plunge harmlessly into the English Channel. The British and the American pilots would make a pass under the bomb and try to explode this device. However, this was not a very good approach, as the exploded bomb would shower fragments into the front of the fighter plane. All the Allied pilots were stumped as to the best way to shoot down these bombs.

There was one pilot (we were told that it was an American) who finally arrived at the solution to this dilemma. The fact that a gyroscope was used to keep the buzz bomb in level flight became an important item towards a solution to this problem. The pilot knew that if anything would upset this level stability the rocket-bomb would fall harmlessly into the sea. He discovered that the safest way to cause the buzz bomb to spiral harmlessly into the channel was to upset this stability. He would fly under the bomb and adjust his flying speed to

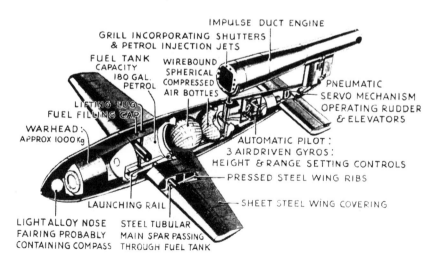

Fig 102. Schematic of a **V-1** rocket bomb.

that of the bomb. He then would put his wing tip under the wing tip of the bomb. The pilot would gently raise his wing tip causing the wing tip of the bomb to rise. Sometimes it would take several tries by the pilot before he would upset the stability of the gyroscope. A large number of these bombs were destroyed in this manner.

These buzz bombs were not very accurate. They were fired from an inverted ski ramp. The British had established an extremely efficient system to determine any impending explosion of the buzz bombs. The advance spotters would note the passing of a plane or a flying bomb as it passed over their specific location. These spotters would report the vital information of time and direction to a central location. This information thus gathered would permit the personnel in the central site to estimate the time and area of the pending explosion. The specific area would then be forewarned concerning the possibility of an explosion. The sounding of sirens or horns would indicate the approximate time before touch down and the following explosion. One blast of the siren or horn was called the blue alert. This indicated that the bomb was some distance away. The second signal was called the yellow alert. This indicated that the bomb was closer but not imminent. The next alarm indicated the red zone alert. This last signal indicated an explosion was very imminent and that every one should take cover. If an air raid shelter was nearby the people should enter the shelter.

A New Dress Causes Injury

These **V-1** bombs had a very peculiar explosive nature. They

Fig 103. V-1 in flight. The launching mechanism is shown just separating from the bomb section, then the rocket would fire.

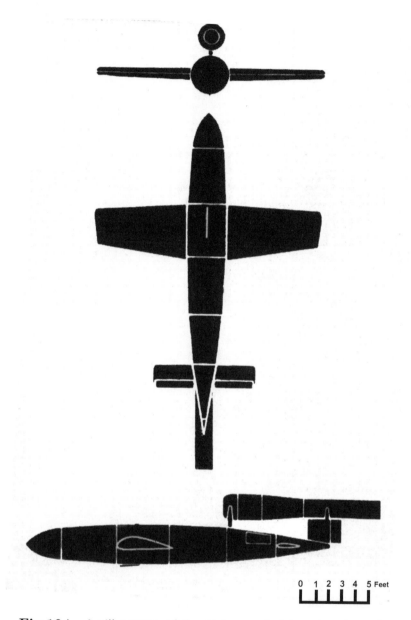

0 1 2 3 4 5 Feet

Fig 104. A silhouette of the flying rocket bomb referred to as the **V-1** (buzz bomb).

were designed to cause a horizontal energy blast. This blast would travel about two feet above the ground. There was a story that was circulated in England relative to this unusual blast. A woman had purchased a new dress and was wearing it for the first time. There was a red alert but she was not near any air raid shelter. The air raid warden told her to lie down on the ground. This woman said she would not get her new dress dirty. She insisted in standing erect. The bomb exploded very close to this area. And this woman was the only person that was injured.

These buzz bombs also had another peculiar trait. The explosion often caused an implosion. I was walking down the middle of a street (we were told that this was the safest area). There were several small, glass-fronted stores on this street. A buzz bomb exploded on the next street. The implosion force of this bomb created a vacuum and the glass of these stores shattered and fell out into the street instead of into the stores. This is the effect of the implosion. I tried to get flat on the ground for the safest position. However, before I could get down I felt a slap on my thighs from the force of the explosion. Fortunately, the force of the blast was weakened at the time it hit me.

A Bomb with a Silent Approach (V-2)

The Germans also developed another secret weapon, a rocket considerably larger than the **V-1**. This **V-2** bomb was also equipped with a warhead. These huge rockets were mounted on their own transporter. Thus they were very mobile. This mobility made it very difficult for the Allied pilots to spot the launch sites. The force of the rocket engine sent this huge bomb skyward. The angle of firing was such that it would come down somewhere in the London area. The speed that was attained in its downward flight was greater than the speed of sound. Therefore, the explosion would occur before you would hear the screeching sound of the oncoming bomb. This resulted in an extremely eerie sensation.

I was visiting the British family of a soldier I met while I was in the British field hospital in North Africa. His family lived in Southall, Middlesex a suburb of London. A **V-2** or a super-sonic rocket exploded nearby. The explosion blew me across the room. I suffered some minor bruises from the impact with the wall.

These bombs were designed to create a degree of fear in the English. There were many fires caused by these weapons. The bombing by the German Luftwaffe also had caused considerable damage. The British did not let these air raid attacks affect their morale. The Germans bombed London and other cities. The plan of the German Luftwaffe had been to break down the English spirit. The war may have been extended if the Germans concentrated their bombing efforts on those factories that produced war products.

Fig 105.

A **V-2** rocket at the manufacturing plant.

This rocket is 26 feet tall.

Fig 106. A **V-2** in flight immediately leaving the mobile launching platform.

Finding Friends

There was a special place we could visit while on shore leave in England. We would enter this military building provided we supplied the proper identification. The person that attended to you would ask you for one name and one name only. The name had to be of an American military person stationed in England. The information that you received in turn would tell you the location of that particular individual.

I used this facility on two separate occasions. The first time I obtained the location of my aunt's nephew. He was stationed near the town of Duxford, and I sent this information to my aunt. She then wrote to her nephew and asked him "How are things in Duxford?" Naturally, he was surprised that his aunt knew where he was located. He had never stated in his letters where he was located. Any information about your location that was sent in letters was automatically censored. The Duxford airfield is presently an aircraft museum featuring World War II airplanes from both the Allies and the Axis.

Fig 107. A picture of the P-47 (Thunderbolt) fighter plane. This plane contained a radial engine, which differed from the P-51 (Mustang) that was previously mentioned which had an in-line engine.

The next time I went to this military facility I wanted to know where an air force friend of mine was stationed. I found where he was located and made plans to go and visit him. We had a very pleasant visit with each other. However, while I was visiting him, a number of the bombers were returning from their attack over Germany. These bombers were B-17 "Flying Forts." You could readily see that most of these bombers were badly damaged. I could see a hole in one of the wings of a plane that was large enough to fit a jeep. The mood at this bomber base was very somber. Shortly after the last bomber had landed a P-47

"Thunderbolt" pilot buzzed the field flying upside down.

He flew past the control tower at a height of about ten feet. It was assumed that this pilot was part of the fighter cover that protected the bombers. The general in charge of this air base was very irate at this "hot shot" pilot.

Fig 108. A photo of a P-51 (Mustang), which was a fast fighter plane. This model of fighter plane was able to provide fighter escort to the bombers flying deep into Germany.

Special LSTs

The events after "D-Day" were somewhat anti-climactic. We continued making trips across the English Channel. One more item of note occurred at the port of Cherbourg.

There was a need to move some of the supplies by rail instead of by truck. The width of the railroad tracks in France was different from those in England. Therefore, a number of railroad cars with the proper track width were assembled. The British solved this dilemma. There were also a number of LSTs fitted with rails inside the tank deck.

The newly assembled railroad cars were put aboard the special LSTs. These LSTs then crossed the channel to Cherbourg. The railroad cars were pulled from the LST directly onto a connecting track to the French railroad. However, before the railroad cars from the LST could be transferred a special device was necessary to facilitate this exchange. This idea saved countless hours in the unloading and subsequent transportation of the military supplies. One railroad car could hold the equivalent contents of several trucks.

The LST was used for another unusual application. A separate

Fig 109. This LST is unloading railroad cars at Cherbourg. Note: this is the same LST that was earlier unloading onto pontoons. The conversion proba- bly took place inside an LSD, again illustrating the flexibility of the ships in the amphibious fleet.

wooden deck was built several feet above the main deck. It extended from the bridge super structure area to the bow. Thus was formed a modified and very small "aircraft carrier." A scout observation (SO) plane could take off from this "carrier." I do not know if the plane could land on this modified LST. A scout observation plane is similar to a Piper Cub plane. It is employed to spot and report enemy movements, activities, positions, gun emplacements, etc. This information was relayed to the artillery units, or aircraft facilities, or ground troops. These units then could take the necessary military action.

Fig 110. Another LST being employed as a railroad car.

Seven or Eleven

Our crew watches were divided into three parts. This usually meant that we would receive liberty once every three crossings. Gambling was very popular with the sailors. It usually took the form of a crap game. There was a game-taking place on board our ship during one of the crossings of the English Channel. There were over 100, five-pound notes in the pot at one time. This is the equivalent of approximately two thousand U.S. dollars. These five-pound British notes were printed on a very flimsy paper. The American GIs had a very uncomplimentary name for this money. I will not print it here.

Sail for Scotland

A change in the above routine occurred near the end of November. We received orders to sail into the Irish Sea and land at the town of Rosneath, Scotland.

I was fortunate to have liberty a few times. There was nothing of interest in Rosneath so our liberty was spent in Glasgow, a short train ride away. I went to Glasgow for my first liberty and wanted to visit the USO. I stopped and asked a Scotsman "Where is the USO?" His answer was as follows; "You go down this street a short ways then you go a little farther. You cannot miss it." I looked a long time before I finally located the USO. The Scotsman's instructions were not very clear. The main street in Glasgow had a very peculiar name. It was called Sauchiehall Street (pronounced sucky hall).

Decommission the LST 351

We were informed that we were going to decommission the ship and turn it over to the British. Rosneath is a short train ride from Glasgow. We were in the port area for several days preparing the ship for the decommission procedure. This procedure meant that during the ceremonies a brand new American flag would be used. The old wind-beaten one was removed. I still have that flag today. It contains only forty-eight stars. Hawaii and Alaska had not attained statehood at the time of this decommissioning. The ceremony took place late in the afternoon. Our crew were all packed and ready to leave. The ceremonies were lengthy but finally completed.

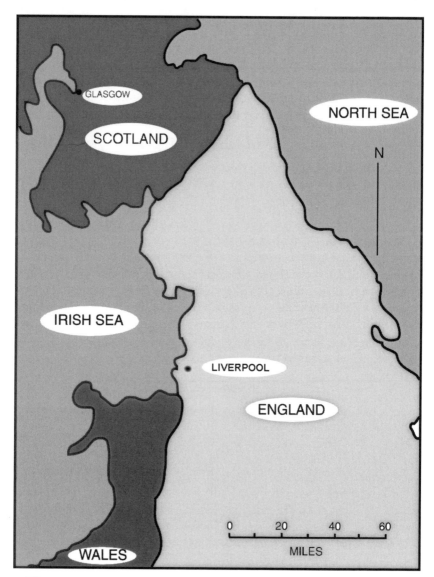

Fig 111. A map of Scotland and England showing the distance from Glasgow to Liverpool.

Homeward Bound

We were put aboard a railroad train with all of our earthly belongings. We traveled into the darkness of the night, and we were not told of our destination. We ultimately reached our destination and told to go aboard a ship in the harbor. Later we heard that we were taken to Liverpool. This is where we boarded the ship. This ship was a former luxury liner and may have been previously named the George Washington. I do not remember the wartime name.

Our crew were some of the last persons to come aboard. It was loaded with American soldiers, sailors, and many casualties. There was not sufficient sleeping space for everyone. Therefore, you slept where and when you could find time and space. I spent considerable time on the signaling bridge. This area became my predominant place to visit and sleep during the crossing. There was not much grumbling on board as we all knew we were sailing for home.

It was during the crossing that we heard about the Battle of the Bulge. Information regarding this historic battle was received by radio. Then announcements were reported over the public address system. We also spent Christmas at sea. Our crossing of the Atlantic Ocean took seven days as compared to the thirty-six days to cross in the other direction. The ocean liner can travel faster than the LST, and at this time there was less concern regarding enemy submarines, therefore no need to zigzag.

Returnees Lighten Their Load

The dawn was beginning to show its light as we were approaching the Statue of Liberty. There was much shouting, whistling, and clapping as the Statue came into view.

Someone on the ship decided he had been carrying his helmet and gas mask for too long a time and felt it was time to put an end to carrying them. He threw his helmet and gas mask into the water, which prompted hundreds of military personnel to follow his example I had scratched the names of all the places I had visited on the plastic liner of my helmet. That helmet with liner and hundreds more are laying at the bottom of New York harbor.

Relating Ones Feelings-Then Silence

We were granted a leave upon our arrival in New York. I was told to report to the Great Lakes Naval Training Center at the end of my leave. These orders were given to me in New York. I was fortunate to get a flight aboard a C-47 from New York to Detroit. The C-47 was designed as a cargo plane but a few were equipped for passenger service. The civilian designation is DC-3. D stood for Douglas and the C for a cargo plane. This is the type of plane that carried the airborne troops for almost every parachute and glider operation around the world. I arrived in Detroit and I hitchhiked to Grand Rapids, as I had in the past.

My aunt Irene arranged for many of the relatives to gather at her place. I answered many questions regarding my experiences. I spoke for five hours and I tried to answer all questions to the best of my ability. That evening I spoke freely and openly. My mother was deaf and unable to keep up with all the conversation. My mother had never heard my voice.

My Aunt Irene knew shorthand and recorded all of this. She later transcribed my five-hour dissertation, making a draft of all the questions and conversations and typed them for my mother to read. My mother kept and treasured this set of papers. These papers were lost many years later when my mother went to live in a nursing home. This was the only time I spoke about my experiences for approximately another ten years.

Later I discovered that this silence was a common occurrence among military personnel who had seen enemy action. It was not evident to me at the time, but as I look back upon my experiences it became apparent to me that there should have been some form of counseling or debriefing of these military persons. The soldiers, sailors, Marines and Air Force persons that met with enemy action should have been encouraged to speak about their experiences and not to hold their feelings within themselves. I realized this, in June of 1994, when I was asked to speak about my experiences to the fourth grade class at the Longacre, Elementary School in Farmington, Michigan. This was the fiftieth anniversary of the allied landing at Normandy. The questions of this fourth grade class were excellent and not one silly question was asked. These children indicated a real interest. I was asked to speak only twenty minutes regarding my military experiences. Their teacher stated that after twenty minutes the students would become bored and restless. The talk lasted for 80 minutes.

The fact that a picture of our ship appeared in the July 1944 issue of the National Graphic magazine aided in the interest of my little talk. Naturally, I brought a copy of this magazine with me and passed it around for all the class to see. It is important that the veterans who served during World War II pass on some of their experiences to the school children of today. This thought should hold for anyone who has been in an armed engagement. There is a national group that is attempting to foster this specific idea. Their theme is "We Shall Remember".

Seasoned Sailors Versus Specialists

The orders I received in New York stated that I was to report to a certain commander at the Great Lakes Naval Training Center. These orders also contained railroad passage from my home in Grand Rapids to the training center. I arrived before the appointed hour and reported to the specific commander. He informed me that I was to become part of a large experimental program. This program took a number of sailors that had seen enemy action and made them company commanders of a fresh batch of raw recruits. The sailor groups that had seen enemy action were pitted against the sports celebrities who were specifically trained to teach the recruits. These sports celebrities were selected because of their potential as role models and also due to their fit physical condition. Some of these trainers were thus protected from assignment to sea duty and the possibility of experiencing enemy action.

The Navy believed that these men were more important as trainers. The program was designed to determine what type of background afforded the best means of training recruits. The results determined that the sailors with war experience made better teachers than the athletes who were specially trained.

One of the things we had to teach the recruits were some songs. Then we would march to the beat of this singing. I taught my company several songs and in some cases the words were of a raunchy nature. One day while we were marching we passed the commander's office. The men did not know that we were passing his office. They broke out in one of the songs but they sang the raunchy version. Naturally, I was called before the commander regarding this specific event. He promptly informed me that the teaching of this type of words to any song was to cease.

Passing of President Roosevelt

I had one hundred and thirty-seven men in my training company. They were referred to as "boots." Thus, the training was called "Boot Camp." It was during this period of training that we were informed of the death of President Franklin Delano Roosevelt. The men were in a very somber mood upon hearing the news.

A month later the end of the war in Europe was declared. The President would have been very elated for this information. There was considerable shouting, whistling, and hugging when we heard this news.

Two in a Berth

My "boot" company graduated. I expected to be assigned another group of "boots" for training. My superior said that I had to wait for further orders. These new orders did not include teaching raw recruits. My commander could not nor would not divulge what these new orders contained. He informed me that I was to stay at the Great Lakes Naval Training Center until I received my orders. He also told me that I could not have any leave.

I was ordered to escort 20 "boots" to an ammunition dump in Lincoln, Nebraska and travel overnight. A Navy bus took us to the train station. We were assigned to berths in accordance with arrangements made between the railroad and the officer making our travel plans. I informed the group that bedtime would be 22:00 (10:00 PM). I decided to make a bed check at approximately 23:00 hours at which time I could account for only 19 of my 20 charges. There was a black woman lying in one of the bunks that had been assigned to one of my sailors. I was really perplexed. I went back and made another bed check. We were traveling in three cars; therefore, it took several minutes to perform this bed check. I found two sailors in the same berth during the second bed check. The navy strictly forbids this situation. I questioned these two sailors about what had happened? They told me that the porter had asked one of the sailors to get out of his bunk. It seems that the porter reserved this particular berth for his friends. I located the porter and had him make other arrangements for his girl friend. The reason that I missed counting the first time was that the sailor was in the head.

The Force Of A Tornado

We finally reached our destination without further problems, arriving at the ammo dump early in the morning. I was to catch the next train back to Chicago, which did not stop in Lincoln, Nebraska until the next morning, so I had to spend the night at the base. The city of Lincoln was some distance from the Naval site. Therefore, I just wandered around the base. It was early evening when the sky became very dark. Rain and hail came down very strongly. The main building was on a slight rise and away from the ammunition sheds. A tornado touched down while I was wandering and wondering. I was contemplating what would be my new orders when I returned to the Great Lakes Center. I was in the main building looking down at some of the ammunition sheds and I saw the tornado pick up one of these sheds and move it several hundred feet. I witnessed, first hand the force and devastation of a tornado. There was debris all over the ground. Fortunately, the main building was not affected. The entire event took only a few minutes. Sailors were sent out after the storm had subsided to cleanup the mess. I had my dinner and sacked in (term for going to bed). I was unable to sleep because the force and the devastation of the tornado were fresh in my mind. I was awakened early in the morning and I had my breakfast. I boarded my train and traveled back to Chicago.

Softball

My commander did not have any further orders for me when I had returned from the ammunition dump. I heard that there was a softball team that needed some players so I spoke to the coach and explained my situation. He said he would be glad to have me on his team until I received my orders. I played several games as a second baseman. I was batting over .400 at the time I heard that Tommy Upton had arrived at Great Lakes.

Tommy Upton

It was during this slack time that there was a recruit beginning his training. This particular man was a former baseball player. There was a Great Lakes baseball team that was under the management of Bob Feller. Mr. Feller heard that there was a baseball playing recruit in camp and wanted him to join the baseball team. This young man was Tommy Upton. His baseball position was shortstop. Base regulations forbade a recruit to move around the camp outside of his restricted area. Therefore, Tommy was not free to go to baseball practice that was located at another section of this huge naval base without an escort.

I volunteered to take Tommy back and forth to baseball practice and the games, since I was still awaiting further orders. This ended my softball games at Great Lakes. I wondered why I had not been assigned to lead another "Boot Company." The only answer I was given was that new orders were forthcoming and they did not include further recruit training. Therefore, I became Tommy Upton's chaperon for the baseball practice and games.

Practicing With The Team

The first few days it was rather boring to sit in the dugout while practice was being conducted. I asked Bob Feller if I could put on a pair of spikes and work out with the team. Bob asked me what position I would like to practice? I replied, "Second base." He agreed to this arrangement. Some of the players on this team were: Walker and Mort Cooper, Johnny Groth, Johnny Gorsica, and Pinky Higgins, all former players from the major leagues.

Batting Against Bob Feller

One day a game was scheduled against a Kansas City team. I do not remember if it was the Blue Jays or the Jay Hawks. The manager of the visiting team said he was a man short and asked if Mr. Feller would permit one of his players to play on his team. Bob Feller wanted to know at what position was the team short? The manager stated that he was missing a man at second base. Feller looked at me and asked if I would like to fill in at second base for the visiting team. I gladly replied affirmatively. Bob Feller was the scheduled pitcher for that day. Thus, I had the privilege of batting against the famous Bob Feller. I batted right-handed and was able to get two hits in four times at bat. The hits were both to right field between the first and the second basemen. I also made a fielding error on that day.

Bob Feller Says Good-bye

A few days later I received my orders. I was to report to Columbia University in New York City for V-5 officers' training. I chaperoned Tommy Upton to the practice field on my last day at Great Lakes. I asked Bob Feller to give me an autographed baseball. He promptly agreed. He gave me a ball after the practice but he was so busy that he did not have time to sign it. I still have that baseball. He wished me good luck on my new venture and said he enjoyed having me work out with the team.

Tommy Upton was later signed by the Yankees but traded to the Washington Senators. I was able to meet again with Tommy when the Senators played against the Detroit Tigers. This meeting took place after we both had been discharged from the Navy. There was considerable reminiscing.

Officer's Training

I had a few days of leave while I was enroute to New York City. It was during this time that the Navy changed the ruling on all V-5 applicants. There would not be any more V-5 programs; rather they would be replaced with V-12 programs. The big difference between these two programs for officer training was that under the V-5 system an applicant would receive a degree in his interested field. It was Engineering in my case. The V-12 program stated that the degree earned would be in Naval Science. The net result was that the majority of the courses would be related to naval sciences instead of the engineering courses I desired. The normal courses in engineering would be more valuable to me in later life than the naval science courses.

Sports

I intended to become active in some sports while I was at Columbia University. I tried out for the tennis team and was accepted. I never did engage in any competitive matches. The competition in tennis against other colleges was usually for the best seven or five team members. Thus, I became a player for practice for the better team members.

I also went out for the football team. The first day of practice we showered, then stepped on the scales. Lou Little, the gravely speaking coach, was looking everyone over as they were weighed. I stepped on the scale and the dial read all of one hundred and thirty-six pounds. Mr. Little looked at me and the number on the dial stated that he thought I was too small to play football. I replied that some of the great players in football were about my size. Lou answered back; "If you can name one small player I will consider you for the team." I responded with the name of Monk Meyer, a quarterback for the Army team. Lou said, OK, you can try out for the football team.

The first few days of practice involved running and calisthenics. The first day that we practiced in complete football gear Lou had an unusual contest. We were to run the length of the football field and be timed in this one hundred yard run. I came in first and my time was 10.4 seconds. Lou Little began to have more confidence in my abilities.

Lou had another exercise for us. We played one-on-one. The man with the ball would attempt to run around or over another man who would try to tackle him. This was done between the five-yard stripes. There were very few players that could tackle me, as I was too quick and shifty for the tacklers to catch me. The situation was reversed; I was the tackler and only a few men could get past me. Lou Little made several favorable comments to me after these two trials.

The Drop Kick, a Lost Art

I was playing around and doing some drop kicking during one of the practice sessions. Lou spotted me and requested that I stay after the regular practice. The regular kicker and I practiced every day on our kicking. He was a place kicker but I was working at both placekicking and the drop kick. Lou told me that the drop kick was becoming a lost art. I was fairly accurate at twenty yards or less. I did not have sufficient strength to kick the ball any farther. My buddy, the place kicker ultimately played professional football for the St Louis Cardinals.

There were two other players that later played professional football. One was Lou Kusserow who played fullback for one of the Canadian teams. The other player who made a name for himself was Gene Rossides. Gene was a very shifty runner and played tailback for Lou Little. I believe that he later played for the New York Giants. Lou Little decided to let me try out for tailback. Lou informed me that there were two other players ahead of me for this position. He asked me if I was interested in this situation. I stated I would gladly give it a try.

Blood Poisoning

It was at one of the practice sessions that a blister formed on my right heel. The trainer put some salve on it. This was on a Saturday afternoon. The next day I had liberty until 20:00 hours (8PM). Another sailor and I went into New York City. We met two young ladies and were strolling through Central Park. My heel was causing some excruciating pain and I began to limp. One of the girls asked me what was the problem. I told her my heel was very sore. She asked me to pull up my pant leg so she could take a look. She stated that she had some nursing experience. There was a red streak half way up to my knee. She promptly informed me that I had blood poisoning and it required immediate attention. I returned to the university and checked in about 15:00 (3 PM). I immediately signed in at the medical facility. The doctor informed me that if I had waited much longer I might have lost my leg. The blister was lanced and I was told that I would be placed on an extensive soaking schedule. They soaked my foot in the hottest water imaginable. I thought that my foot was burning. I do not know what was more painful, the hot water or the blood poisoning.

This went on for about three days. The doctor informed me that most of the blood poisoning had been extracted and I would be discharged in two or three more days. I was sitting up in bed and one of my sailor friends was passing by in the hall. He came in and asked where had I been for the past several days. He said that I was listed as AWOL. I told him that I had been in the hospital since Sunday afternoon. No sailor returns from liberty five hours early, except in emergencies, so no one thought to check the sign-in sheet for a 3 PM. Return.

However, the records were examined and the "powers-that-be" realized that I had checked in on time and that I was not AWOL. The medical records (which were examined after my discharge), indicated that I had an infection in the right ear. This is an illustration of the efficiency of maintaining Naval medical records.

This week in the hospital put me behind with football practice. Lou Little said he was sorry but he was going to put me at another position. He asked me to play pulling guard on offense and guard on defense. That is the position at which I practiced. I was on the reserve team and we had a game scheduled. I think it was against Syracuse or Lafayette. I played my guard position on both offense and defense.

I was on defense for the first series of plays and was playing opposite a giant tackle. I was a brazen young man and felt that I could accomplish almost any thing. I said to myself "I can run right through this tackle." The ball was snapped and I tried to go through the tackle. The next thing I knew, I was flat on my rump and four or five feet back of where I started. So much for my bravado.

I realized that I had to use my quickness to get around that big tackle. I feinted in one direction and went around him in another direction. This proved to be very successful. I was able to tackle the runner in the backfield several times using this maneuver. I completely missed a tackle after breaking through into the backfield. The coach pulled me out and asked why I had missed an apparent easy tackle. I was put back into the game after a few plays had been completed.

More Contract Bridge

We played a considerable amount of contract bridge while I was attending Columbia University. This became our favorite pastime while we were in school. One of the other sailors became my partner. He was an excellent bridge player but was very aggressive in his bidding. However, we made more hands than we lost.

Naval Science Teacher

There was one instructor that trained us in naval machinery and gunnery. There was one reference that he made concerning the attempt to determine if something was hot. He stated that if you want to test the temperature of something you use the back of your little finger on your opposite hand. If you were right handed then you would test the item with the back of your little finger on your left hand. If you should burn yourself, then that is the part of your hand you use the least and that part that is not so easily bumped.

Time in New York City

I always went into New York City for my liberties. I attempted to do as much sightseeing as possible. There was one time that I was given overnight liberty. I had seen Lily Pons at a performance at the Radio City Music Hall. Oscar Levant, was playing the piano. It was rather late and I was hungry. I entered a small restaurant and ordered a double order of fried eggs. The owner heard this and he questioned my request. He said that a single order consisted of two eggs, two pieces of toast, two sausages, two pancakes, and some hash browns. He asked me again, was I sure I wanted a double order? I replied yes. He stated that if I could eat a double order then I could eat free at his restaurant any time I wished. I finished that double order without any difficulty. Naturally I took advantage of his kind offer several more times. The owner of this establishment and I had many pleasant chats.

Liberty in New York City

An airplane flew directly into the Empire State building, almost at a right angle. The plane was embedded in the side of the structure and just suspended there. It was during one of my visits to New York City that I saw the airplane. It was a weird sight to see the airplane sticking out from this tall building.

There were free tickets available to the servicemen in New York. These could be for a performance at the Radio City Music Hall, or for a movie or a stage play or for a baseball game. I always tried to obtain tickets for the Music Hall. I enjoyed the musical performances and the "Rockettes". There were times that all the tickets had been taken. It was on these occasions that I opted to go ice-skating at the Radio City Building's outdoor skating rink. I saw baseball games at the New York Giants; Polo Grounds, the Brooklyn Dodgers', Ebbets Field, and also at Yankee Stadium.

War Ends

The war was over. The war ended on August 15, 1945. This later became known as "V-J" day. (The celebration for "V-E" was nothing as compared to the celebration in New York City corresponding to "V-J" day). There was singing, dancing, shouting, paper falling from almost every window downtown, and people hugging each other. The noise was deafening. The jubilation was beyond comprehension. Times Square became a madhouse with everyone kissing and hugging each other. There was considerable joy and happiness.

The official ending of the war was declared when the Japanese signed an unconditional surrender aboard the Battleship USS Missouri on September 2, 1945.

Request Discharge

The end of the semester was approaching and I desired to know what the requirements were for me to obtain a commission. I was informed that I would be committed to the Navy for an additional two and a half years. This would include my university training and some time as an officer. This did not suit my desires, especially, that I would not be receiving many courses in engineering. My length of service and the fact that I was supporting my widowed mother gave me enough points for a discharge. Points were counted based upon length of service, time overseas, the number of enemy engagements, and extra points if you were supporting a person at home.

Therefore, I requested my discharge to take effect at the end of the present semester. I was released from Columbia University and was sent to the Great Lakes Naval Training Center for my formal discharge from the United States Naval Reserve. I was given my honorable discharge papers on October 16, 1945. I had completed forty months of service in the United States Navy Reserve and left the Navy as a Signalman 3rd class.

<u>Debriefing</u>

There is a situation that I have discussed with several other military personnel. It was mentioned above but I believe that it is sufficiently important to be repeated. Those service persons that had seen enemy action should be encouraged to speak about their experiences and their feelings. This should be done as soon as possible after their discharge. If the person has been wounded and subsequently enters into a hospital, then he should be encouraged to speak before he is discharged from the hospital.

The service persons will not want to talk but these people should be encouraged to speak. An extremely difficult situation, therefore, exists. The person needs to speak but his experiences are of such a nature that he or she does not wish to speak. There are military people today, fifty years later, that do not wish to recall nor mention what had happened to them. Harboring these memories does not lend itself to a good and pleasant mental condition. Although I speak of military persons and their experiences, this should also include any war correspondent or non-military personnel that may have witnessed enemy action.

I spoke at my aunt's house but did not wish to express any of my thoughts and feelings for at least another ten years. Keeping these thoughts to myself kept festering my insides. This was a common occurrence to each of the members of the service to whom I spoke.

The Little Recognized
Amphibious Sailor

There is an anonymous poem that sums up the meaning of the amphibious sailor. It is as follows:

THE AMPHIBIOUS MAN

You've heard of the Air Force
And the Marine Paratroops
But think as hard as you can
Though you've heard of the Army
And of other groups
Have you heard of the Amphibious Man?

The Amphibious Gob is a real rugged sort,
But unlike the fleet, he has no homeport;
Goes where he is needed
Does what he can
This poor orphan sailor;
The Amphibious Man.

You might be a battleship sailor
From a cruiser, or off a "tin-can".
May be fresh out of boot camp,
Or perhaps a second cruise man.
They pick the men at random,
How else can they provide?
A few might choose the duty,
But they mostly were Shanghaied.

You've heard plenty of the Navy
Of ships both fore and aft,
But we'll bet a pretty penny
You've heard least of the Amphib's landing craft.
They've built a few already,
And they're building plenty more,
For they've got to have the LSTs
To win this doggone war.

They're loaded from the transports
In the middle of the night,
And always keep their rendezvous
Can't even show a light.
Find their way in the darkness,
And land up on the shore,
Tho' bombs discharge their cargo,
They go right back for more.

Bringing in the first wave
Doesn't end the job.
For the troops upon the beach
Can't live without this Gob.
He brings in reinforcements
And everything they use,
His job is full of danger,
But he never makes the news.

For when the beach is taken
And the radio starts to tell
You'll hear of the Marines and Army,
And how they went thro' hell;
You'll thrill to the front page stories
Of their heroic job
But you'll never hear a word
Of the poor Amphibious Gob!

And when this war is over,
And he's back in civilian life.
How in the hell will he explain
To his kiddies and his wife?
They knew he was in the Navy
But he's subject to a gyp.
He's just an orphan sailor
A Gob without a ship!

Summary

I earned five medals in the war: the American Campaign, the Admiral's Commendation (a special meritorious award for my performance during "D-Day", the Purple Heart for being wounded in the line of duty (during an air raid at Lake Bizerte in North Africa), the European Theater of Operations with a Silver Star to indicate being in five major engagements, and the Victory Medal. The five major engagements were: the enemy action in North Africa and the Invasions of Sicily, Salerno, Anzio, Normandy, which is better known as "D-Day". I was participated in four invasions before I was twenty-two years old.

The above writing is accurate to the best of my memory. Most of the story was written after an elapse of 50 years. There are probably some errors. Some of the anecdotes were inserted between the paragraphs at the appropriate place. There was no diary nor were there any notes. Almost all of the above anecdotes are the result of my memory.

Sources of Information

This paper was written from varied sources of information. Many occurrences were actually observed by me. The troops that returned with us to our base often supplied information regarding their experiences or observations. Many times one would meet a sailor or a soldier at a USO function and exchange experiences.

There have been considerable books written on various subjects relative to the war. One source of information that has been utilized is the numerous documentaries that have been shown on various television channels. Known sources of certain specific information is also acknowledged.

It is extremely difficult to cite exact sources. Many books and stories were read. The History Television Programs were watched extensively. A word here or a paragraph there may have reminded me of an old memory. No diary was kept, no notes were taken, and many of the anecdotes are brought forth after fifty years.

Some of the books that were read are:

Ninety and Nine by William Brinkley

The Longest Day by Cornelius Ryan

The Dawn of D-Day by David Howarth

World War II, A 39 volume set by Time-Life Books

Pictorial History of World War II published by Wm. H Wise Co.

The National Geographic Magazine, July 1944 issue

Pegasus Bridge June 6, 1944 by Stephen E. Ambrose

Anzio by Wynford Vaughan-Thomas

The Valiant Years by Winston Churchill

Great Battles of World War II by John J Tarrant

Kasserine Pass by Martin Blumenson

Big Men of the Little Navy by Paschal E. Kerwin, O.F.M.

The Amphibious Man, Amphibious Training Base,
    Camp Bradford, N.O.B., Norfold, VA

About the Author

Mr. Jagers was born in Chicago, Illinois in 1922. He later moved to Grand Rapids, Michigan. He attended Aquinas College in Grand Rapids for two years before enlisting in the Navy in June 1942.

He married his wife Rose, in Chicago in June 1946. They moved to Detroit, Michigan where Mr. Jagers graduated from the University of Detroit in 1950 with a degree in Chemical Engineering. He received his Masters Degree in Chemical Engineering from Wayne State University in 1957. He worked for the Chrysler Corporation and retired in 1979.

He has done considerable volunteer tutoring for ten years. In 1997 he received the prestigious "Friend of Education Award" from the Farmington School District for his work with the school children.

He has two daughters, Kathleen and Beverly;
one son, Richard; and one grandson, Jeremy.

He has traveled extensively to more than 40 countries.
He is active in the Society of Automotive Engineers.

He presently lives in Farmington, Michigan, USA.

Picture Credits

Author – Fig 9, 12, 46, 52, 55, 57, 59, 60, 63, 66, 75, 78, 87, 101, 111

Booklet – Fig 79

German Publication – Fig 89, 90, 91, 92, 99, 100, 102, 103, 104, 105, 106

History Channel – Fig 8

Imperial Museum – Fig 39

London Daily – Fig 81, 82, 83, 84, 85

Maps – Fig 53, 54, 61, 64, 65, 74, 80, 86, 88

Poster – Fig 97

U.S. Air Force – Fig 11

U.S. Army – Fig 2, 22, 28, 36, 41, 43, 48, 72, 98

U.S. Coast Guard – Fig 19, 21, 29, 31, 34, 35, 40, 69, 109, 110

U.S. Navy – Fig 1, 4, 5, 6, 13, 14, 15, 16, 17, 18, 20, 23, 24, 25, 26, 27, 30, 32, 42, 45, 56, 62, 67, 68, 70, 71, 73, 76, 77, 93, 94, 95, 96

U.S. Marine Corps – Fig 3, 33, 38, 44

U.S. Signal Corp – Fig 49

Valliant Years – Fig 47, 58

World War II Aircraft – Fig 7, 10, 37, 50, 51, 107, 108

Figure Index

INDEX

INDEX

To order additional copies of **Whales of World II**, send check or money order for **$18.45** ($14.95 + $3.50 S&H) to:

Robert B. Jagers
35509 Heritage Lane
Farmington, MI 48335

Email: **BJagers@greatid.com**